Searching SALMON FALLS

Tracing the Path of a High Desert Creek

MIKE COTHERN

Thunderhead Press
P. O. Box 5244
Twin Falls, ID 83301

Grateful acknowledgment is given to the *Twin Falls Times-News*, which originally published a five-part series featuring various segments of the Salmon Falls Creek drainage

Cover and interior design by KUHN Design Group | kuhndesigngroup.com
Cover and interior photographs by the author

Printed in the United States of America

ISBN 979-8-218-04294-3

Library of Congress Control Number: 2022914513

www.mikecothern.com

Dedicated to

Beth, who has shared more trails with me
than everyone else combined

Keegan, our historian with a world view

Mom and Dad, gone but whose thirst for
wild places still lives inside me

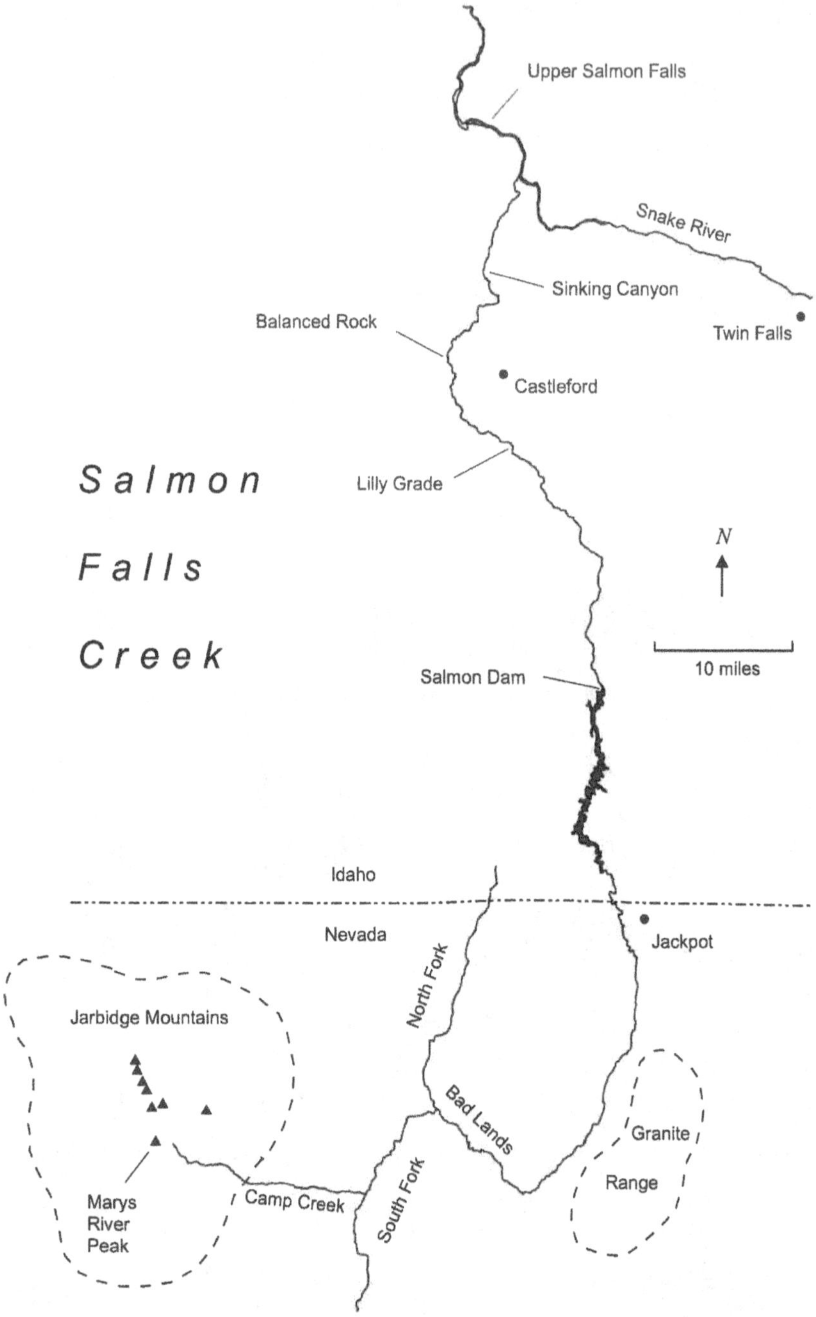
Upper Salmon Falls
Snake River
Sinking Canyon
Balanced Rock
Twin Falls
Castleford
Salmon Falls Creek
Lilly Grade
N
10 miles
Salmon Dam
Idaho
Nevada
Jackpot
North Fork
Jarbidge Mountains
Bad Lands
Granite Range
Marys River Peak
Camp Creek
South Fork

Chapter 1

JANUARY 2

Even after being slowed by the predawn fog, the drive from my home to the canyon takes little more than ten minutes. As I ease down Lilly Grade the mist breaks up, however, and while rounding a sharp curve the beam of the pickup's headlights is lost in the dark abyss. After crossing Salmon Falls Creek and maneuvering back up the other side, the departure of a faint two-track from the main road points me into the desert plain. I follow that path for a hundred yards before taking another that leads me back toward the canyon rim.

I stop and shut the lights off, but leave the engine running. While it still might be a little dark to start walking, what I really desire is to soak up some more of the cab's heat before venturing out into the fifteen-degree air. I inventory my pack one last time, linger for a few more minutes, and step out into the cold.

I scan the western sky and enjoy the ebbing shine of the last few stars and a single planet. When I drop my gaze to the horizon, a small herd of deer grabs my attention. A standoff ensues and we spend a moment checking each other out before I begin to walk. Progress is soon halted when I near the lip of the canyon and am offered another scene by the breaking dawn.

Back across the gorge, the silver fog serves as a cloak to hide the farm country that I just drove through. The edge of the cloud seems hung up along the opposite rim, but as I stand and watch, it becomes obvious that the scene is not static. As the mass slowly pulls away, the canyon's sharp edge appears to tear away giant clumps of vapor. Now on their own, these fog fragments are left suspended inside the great void.

After marveling at that spectacle, my focus pulls back to this side of the canyon. Hoarfrost covers the sagebrush and bunchgrasses that surround me. The thick ice crystals offer proof that the fogbank blanketed my position for most of the night before slowly drifting away. The satisfaction of simply looking around only lasts for so long before the camera is pulled out of my day pack. I compose a few photographs in hopes of capturing both the nearby vegetation and the distant, partly obscured landscape. After the sun peeks over the horizon and adds some golden light, I trip the camera's shutter several more times. Bare fingers soon begin to feel the effects of the biting cold and my hands slip back inside gloves.

Before resuming my hike I take one final glance back and see that the mule deer, ears held erect, continue to monitor me. They seem deserving of an explanation for my intrusion, but I'm not sure how easy it might be to fully explain motives. My desire to simply share this area with them would be a good place to start, but there is another stirring that I must attend to. Around the canyon's next bend a spot on the rim will offer me not only a fuller view of the landscape, but perspective into my past.

Hiking that half mile warms me enough to forget about the frigid air. I stop at my observatory, move as close as possible to the edge of the canyon, and absorb the scene. The cliff below me drops vertically for a hundred feet and then abruptly ends at a pile of boulders. At one time those basalt blocks were connected to the stone where I stand. As the rimrock weathered and cracked, pieces separated from the mother rock and were launched downward into the growing rubble pile. In some spots the slope, which angles steeply from the foot of the cliff to the canyon bottom, is covered with strips of the talus. In other places where a thin layer of soil remains, the same plants that accompanied me up here have gained a foothold.

The mix of vegetation and boulders stretches down several hundred feet more in elevation. The toe of the slope then levels out just before meeting the creek. This ribbon of ground serves as the most critical part of the landscape, at least for humans, by providing just enough space to hike along the bottom of the canyon. Often without much of a trail, the corridor must be shared with more boulders, shrubs, and junipers that crowd the creek. Progress is made at a deliberate pace.

I first stepped into the gorge while accompanying my father on a duck hunt. Ten years old and too young to carry a shotgun, I took up the third and final place in line behind hunter and dog. I remember few details about our hunt downstream along the creek and the return trip back up to Lilly Grade, but the rugged land left its impression on me. And even then I grasped the value of living so close to such a wild place.

The canyon repeatedly drew me back into its fold over the next ten years. The outings were shared most often with family and friends, but I also began to appreciate the appeal of exploring solo. The harvest was never bountiful. We dropped a few mallards that flushed off the creek during fall and winter excursions and watched our retrievers work. We pulled medium-sized trout and bass from its water when the warmth of spring made the place feel a little less daunting. Even with the destination only a half-dozen miles from home, the excursions occurred no more than a couple times a year. The effort required to carefully descend into the canyon, scramble through its obstacle course, and then climb out limited the frequency of those trips. The difficult nature of the gorge not only added to the unique experience of each journey, but kept nearly everyone else away.

I reflect on those outings as I stand and gaze down into the canyon. I listen to the creek as it pushes through a stretch of boulders and imagine the whisper of "There they are!" before making a crouched stalk toward ducks or the louder pronouncement of "Got one!" as a fish is fooled. If any place on earth speaks to me, it is this canyon that houses Salmon Falls Creek.

My father introduced me to several pieces of this deep fissure that slices through mostly public land in the southern Idaho desert. And so besides bearing witness to this magnificent chasm and reliving some old experiences, I have shown up to honor him by completing a trip that we discussed but never attempted. Our dream consisted of hiking through the bottom of the canyon from Lilly Grade downstream to Balanced Rock in a single day. The attempt would be made as a duck hunt since that was the only reason, save one, that we entered the canyon together. But it would also have to take place in the fall before the arrival of snow hindered progress and the days became too short.

The journey failed to materialize during my teenage years. The University of Idaho then pulled me away from home and limited our chance for a shared adventure. At the same time, Dad's worsening arthritis made an epic march through the gorge unlikely. When I reached the age of twenty-one, however, any window of opportunity slammed shut. A midair collision with another airplane ended his life and that of my brother Bill's.

While New Year's Day was yesterday, I had not thought of my current trip as tied to a resolution. But perhaps it is. I do hope to fulfill a dream that we once shared, and my plan includes my mother picking me up at Balanced Rock after an all-day, one-way journey. There is a commitment—and resolve. So be it. I will fudge a bit by not carrying a gun and remaining above the canyon rather than inside it, but I think Dad would understand. Besides being limited by the amount of daylight, I doubt that my body could now handle what we had once visualized. Since my own arthritis issues forced me into one hip replacement ten years ago and with the other one needing work in the next year or two, the fifteen-mile challenge through the canyon's interior sounds nearly impossible.

As I move downstream along the rim, the sun continues on its short, winter parabola across the sky behind me. On the opposite side of the canyon, the fogbank continues to drift off to the north. Its departure exposes a handful of the farmland's outlying homesteads, the closest that lie a mile away. Bare deciduous trees clustered around homes and outbuildings bounce the sunlight off their frosty coverings. The countryside wakens. The drone of a front loader, likely moving hay or silage for cattle, reverberates across the frozen landscape. The noise of other machinery occasionally floats across the gulf that I parallel, a reminder again of the abrupt transition from civilization to wildness.

Over there a network of paved roads laid out on square-mile grids comprises an irrigated Eden that inspired the name of Magic Valley. Its labyrinth of cropland, road corridors, and small towns extends far to the north and east. From this side and in the opposite directions, however, one could walk a hundred miles toward Nevada or Oregon and intersect only one paved road each way. That I tread on the wild side of this canyon, along the edge of what some people perceive as empty wasteland, brings me contentment. But while the contrasts between landscapes across the Snake River Plain are engaging, nothing can compete with the dramatic cut in the earth's crust that unfolds in front of me.

My past encounters, perhaps three dozen, with the canyon landscape of Salmon Falls Creek have concentrated on only a fraction of the total amount that the drainage offers. A topographic map's tight contour lines depict the jagged cut that begins just south of the Idaho-Nevada line and runs nearly from one end of Twin Falls County to the other. A straight-line measurement from roughly Jackpot to the Snake River puts that distance at around sixty miles. Trying to account for all the bends in the canyon as it slices mostly north, but a little west, makes measuring its path tricky, but that length is likely half again as much. Salmon Falls Creek's inaccessible nature also becomes apparent when another search of the map reveals that only three roads cross the gorge. Assuming I do make my way to the crossing at Balanced Rock this afternoon, I will have seen two of those in a single day.

The canyon's other traverse occurs about twenty straight miles upstream where a single-lane road runs across Salmon Dam. The concrete poured into the canyon a hundred years ago caused a dramatic change to the creek's downstream journey. While the dam was constructed to divert all water for irrigation and with no intention to allow any to pass, enough leaked around the structure to maintain a minimal yet perennial stream. Springwater that enters near Lilly Grade crossing warms the creek enough to keep it from freezing over as it meanders to the river.

I contemplate today's flow and wonder about its pre-dam presence. What would it have been like to see the chocolate current of an unimpeded spring runoff and listen to the roar of wild water? Or go back even further when snow and ice ruled the region's high country and bear witness to the glacial runoff pouring from the creek's main sources in the Jarbidge Mountains? Those flows did the real carving of this canyon, eroding it down to the four-hundred-foot depth that I see here, or to six hundred in some places upstream.

As I continue to look at the canyon, however, my thoughts shift from the erosive forces and material washed downstream to what remains and is now exposed. Another geological story, this one much older, speaks of volcanoes. Not the iconic cone-like hills or mountains that might expel all sorts of things like ash and gases and smoke and rock with explosive force, but the almost unnoticeable rises that on a map are simply labeled as buttes. Lava oozed from these shield volcanoes for long periods and covered the land for miles with a thin coating of basalt. Tens or hundreds of thousands of years later, another eruption might occur and add its flow over the top of the previous event. The end result reminds me of looking at a stack of pancakes at eye level. From my side of the canyon rim, I count ten different layers on the opposite side that total about 150 feet deep. The flows represent the latest chapter in a time line helping to explain how the earth's crust was constructed.

And so I work my way downstream carrying thoughts of both a distant geological past and my own recent history of the creek and canyon. Occasionally I wander away from the rim with the intent to make better time by either finding a less rocky course or taking a more direct line to the next bend. My attempts are short-lived since the gorge, serving almost as a black hole, pulls me back to the edge.

As I check out the scene after each return, the creek seizes my attention first. My eyes, predictably enough, search for ducks. A few live here year-round, but many are migrant mallards from the north that stop over during the winter and find the combination of open water and nearby harvested cornfields too inviting to leave. Through binoculars I spy on birds scattered in groups ranging from a pair to perhaps twenty. Some remain loyal to one locale and occasionally bob beneath the surface of the water to feed on snails in the shallows. Solitary birds are often spotted only after an infrequent quack or the V of a wake gives them away. Waterfowl gathered on small pools lying between fast water and where junipers offer cover are the last to be located.

Even though I seldom fire a shotgun anymore, it's hard not to look at the ducks with a hunter's eye. The canyon just holds too much of the past between the creek, birds, and me. I critique their locations and imagine what flocks might be vulnerable to a stalk using the brush and rocks as cover. After a while the binoculars are tucked back underneath my jacket. The primal urge to pursue will remain unfilled.

The sight and sound of ducks and water brings forth more. I cannot recall many specific instances of a successful stalk, an accurate shot, or a fruitful retrieve. Those events took place but too long ago, and often enough given the sheer number of outings, that they arise more as a feeling than crisp recollections. Most memorable are those occasions when not everything, or even anything, came together in a satisfying way. I can never forget the time my brother Pat and I, as teenagers, together went through at least two-dozen shells and came home with only three birds. The disapproving look from my dog as we repeatedly failed to give her the command of "Fetch!" now brings me nothing but a smile.

Other hunts never had a chance to play out. While the entrance fee for engaging this wild landscape came in large doses of hard work and sweat, along with a few bruises, sometimes the price was a little more costly than bargained for. One trip concluded within ten minutes after leaving the pickup when I slipped in the snow during a steep descent into the canyon. Within seconds of mashing my thumb between my gun and a rock while breaking my fall, I looked at the already-swelling result and said to my son, "I think we better go home." Another awkward spill flipped me and my then year-old replaced hip down onto another snow-covered rock, resulting in a painful limp back up and out of the canyon. Crossing the creek on boulders glazed with ice while hanging on to a gun never ended with more than a pair of wet feet, but I can still feel the anxiety.

Even the hunting dogs that accompanied us were not immune to the unforgiving nature of the wild chasm. On different occasions two of our black Labradors encountered porcupines. Returning from the tangle of shrubs, trees, and rocks adjacent to the creek, the retrievers produced nothing from their search but a mouthful of quills.

Reliving those mishaps leaves me content to stay up here where the hazards are few and I can simply walk the rim. The memories come as I look at the landscape and reunite with family, friends, and dogs—some still living, others now ghosts. While technically alone, I feel the company of a collection of spirits.

By late morning unfamiliar territory inside the canyon greets me. Confined in the past to a handful of miles in either direction from Lilly Grade, no stories exist to tie me to this novel landscape. And even though I can place my position on the map by matching the bends of the canyon, little across the far side looks familiar either. The edge of the fogbank has moved off several miles, but a small rise still blocks my view of much farmland. The few homesteads that are visible cannot be easily identified due to this unique perspective, and the fact that my internal compass seems to be off about thirty degrees does not help.

The disconnect is likely made worse by my expectation to more easily orient myself up here on top. In the bottom of the canyon, knowing exactly where I am rarely plays into the experience. All the standard landmarks found above the rim are absent. No conventional horizon exists, and true north means little. Only two directions exist: upstream and downstream. Isolated in the canyon's depth, no reason exists to merge the gap between what is wild and what is not.

My slight disorientation is compounded when I enter an area burned by a wildfire two summers ago. Seeing the inferno's aftermath along the rim, below me, and far to the west comes as a shock—even though I knew the burn was here. The fire started a few miles away when a thunderstorm fired a lightning bolt into the earth and ignited July-dry vegetation. Burning over the course of ten days, the Kinyon Road Fire scorched 235,000 acres. The event was the latest in a number of large, erratic range fires that have occurred in the region over the last ten years due in part to a gradual shift toward a warmer and drier climate.

This one rolled down into the canyon, climbed up the east side, and then dashed to the edge of farmland before being subdued. Most of the steep slopes that extend down to the creek are stripped of vegetation. Along lengthy stretches of creek corridor the thick undergrowth has vanished and only skeletons of once-mighty junipers remain. In other spots where the flames were less intense, a scattering of live evergreens still stand amidst groves that while not torched outright, were still subjected to enough heat that their now-brown needles confirm their death.

My route offers no choice but to step into the burn. On one short stretch where I can scramble below the canyon's false rim, I climb over drifts created by a wind-driven brew of snow mixed with a disconcerting amount of ash and soil. Visions pop into my head of the dark clouds that gusted off the desert over the last two summers and could easily be seen from ten miles away. I look again back to the west and see the source of those ominous events. Little plant life remains to protect the bare ground. Even during a winter snowstorm, the land will move.

Besides considering what the wind rips from the plain, I wince when thinking about the erosion caused by rain or snowmelt moving down into the canyon and the soil being carried into the creek. Having lent a critical eye toward soil erosion from the perspective of first a farmer and now a public servant who works with landowners trying to prevent their own loss, I would like to drop down and investigate further. How much soil is being displaced? What types of plants are coming back? What does the future hold?

But in addition to satisfying an objective curiosity, something more personal moves me. I want to stand next to the junipers, touch their charred trunks, and pay my respects. My impulse cannot be acted on, however, since I cannot justify such a major delay. Any mourning today will take place up here from a distance. Wanting to escape the burn and look at something else, I push on but the dismal scene keeps unfolding.

Around noon I reach the day's most anticipated destination where another canyon appears out of the desert and joins mine. Devil Creek's course that begins near the Nevada border is less dramatic, but quickly deepens over the final half mile to reach the same level of Salmon Falls Creek. I walk to the point where the canyon rims meet and sit on an obliging rock. There cannot be a better lunch spot for miles.

The opportunity to stare down into the pair of chasms boosts my morale. The delight gained from soaking up this view tempers the fact that the burn still tarnished most of the area below. Some key spots escaped the flames, however, and I am encouraged to see a string of live junipers along the dry and rocky Devil Creek channel. The meeting of the two drainages also marks a disruption in the narrow gorge that I have become accustomed to following. Their confluence has opened the country up and doubled my canyon's rim-to-rim width. I again fantasize about climbing down and exploring the jumbled basin. After fifteen minutes of eyeing the inviting landscape below, I try to push away all thoughts not related to forward progress. I'm not completely successful, however, until I make a pact with myself to return someday.

My map informs me that I have walked about eight miles along the canyon rim with about a half dozen remaining. That's six miles, of course, if I could flap my arms and fly across this tributary canyon, land on the other side, and resume my exploration of Salmon Falls Creek. Instead I retreat back to the south and check out a couple of false leads where the basalt cliff turns crumbly and lures me down. Each time the attempt is aborted when I reach a sheer drop from a secondary rim. It does not take much near-vertical relief to turn me back; those days when I possessed nimble feet, limber joints, and the confidence to do much intense solo scrambling are long gone.

After working upstream for a half mile to where the canyon's topography and depth are not so imposing, a more promising spot reveals itself. I weave down through a pocket of unburned sagebrush and talus piles. A controlled skid down a steep slope burned bare then delivers me to the bottom.

I find two sets of deer tracks pressed into the moist soil and follow their meander up the Devil Creek channel. Giving up on the doe and fawn after fifty yards, I ascend an open hillside that shows promise of leading me out of the canyon. When the basalt lava flows close in on me and my route begins to look questionable, I discover a faint trail that appears to hold the same hoofprints from before. Did I abandon them too soon? After concluding that these animals know far more about a way out than me, I once again shadow their path. It eventually vanishes into more rocky terrain near the top, but by then I spy a break in the rim, crawl up through it, and return to flat ground.

Instead of heading directly back to Salmon Falls, I angle away from the side canyon and gain a few feet in elevation that results in a better look to the west. More country has been touched by fire, but beyond that my view is blocked by a hill that is a couple miles in width but only a few hundred feet high. While not impressive, Devil Creek Butte represents one of those long-dead shield volcanoes. The low rise is likely responsible for much of the basalt flows witnessed this morning—including those that I just navigated while crossing the drainage with the same name.

My course bends back toward the main canyon and again places me along its rim. An hour of walking then propels me beyond the charred landscape that has troubled me for almost five miles. This stretch of canyon continues to offer more unfamiliar territory, but my outing's novelty has begun to wear off. Ducks scattered along the creek are now of little interest, and I have begun to acknowledge the protest coming from my knees and hips. And while the canyon remains my focal point, I find myself checking out the countryside across from it more often.

I study my map and look through the binoculars to confirm that a dairy and several houses and sheds off in the distance are now where my mind thinks they should be. I perk up a little more when I observe the hint of a crease running from the edge of farmland and into the canyon. Unseen from my vantage point, a paved road tucked down inside that fold crosses the creek, ascends a short but steep grade, and passes near Balanced Rock. Prompted by the plan to meet my mother there, I pull my phone from my day pack and give her a call. She affirms that she is still coming and will arrive just before sundown.

After checking the map once more to confirm my position, I resolve to stop less and instill my stride with some of that spring from earlier in the morning. That intention only lasts for a few steps when, while taking one last look at my phone to note the time, I trip over a small clump of sagebrush. My face plant fortunately occurs in open, semi-thawed ground and the impact is fairly benign. I push myself up and look around out of reflex, but of course there is not another living soul within a couple of miles. With the joke on me, I utter a two-syllable chuckle and then realize the sound is the first one out my mouth all day.

The mishap doesn't seem so funny when I fail to find my phone that was launched into the air. I remain on all fours and crawl around for a few minutes examining the ground. When the still-opened flip phone is found hanging high in the branch of another sagebrush plant, I laugh at myself a second time.

Now in a race with both my mother and the falling sun, I angle away from the day's companion and spend the last hour walking cross-country toward Balanced Rock. I arrive at the landmark, which stands a half mile from the creek, just before Mom. During my final few moments of solitude, I have little chance to even contemplate the rock looming above me on the hillside. It seems odd to have walked all day toward my destination and then give the iconic formation so little time and deference. After I slip into the warm car and we begin to drive away, I find myself hoping for a quick return.

Chapter 2

JANUARY 31

Almost a month later I show up again at the parking lot below Balanced Rock but still with no plan to visit the local attraction. Since my previous hike ended in a hurry and diverted me from a landscape distinctly unlike the first dozen miles, it felt like my journey had gone unfinished. With a desire to rectify that outcome and celebrate my birthday from the day before, one way to address both seemed obvious. I would make a short loop by walking upstream through the canyon and then returning along the last stretch of rim missed earlier.

A strong wind pushes me toward the gorge as I walk down the pavement. The breeze reflects a welcome shift from the weather that lately has been not only dull, but at times miserable. With a high-pressure ridge dominating the region for nearly all of January, a deflected jet stream had carried the potential for needed moisture northward. What did we get out of it? Nothing but a prolonged inversion marked by haze, or more often, dense fog. Two days earlier, however, the stubborn mass and its chilled, stagnant air were muscled out by a powerful front and sent eastward. The new weather system even anointed us with a half inch of rain—the most precipitation delivered since September. On the heels of that storm, today's brisk air and aqua sky invigorate me.

I stop once to turn around, face the stiff breeze, and take one last look up at Balanced Rock. The iconic feature sits away from the main canyon and resides at the upper end of a string of rock monuments that stretch down to the creek and then back up the other side. Some of the formations rise over a hundred feet and appear to stand guard above the intersection of creek and road. The arrangement of stone at the crossing inspired the naming of the nearest town, Castleford, which lies only a few miles away.

While the rhyolite here, like that of the basalt upstream, is of a volcanic nature, the two types have significant differences. The stacked layers of dark gray rock that I observed three weeks ago sparked my imagination in terms of a geological time line, but these older rust-colored compositions provoke me in a much different way. Their abrupt, random nature that has resulted in a variety of shapes and sizes belies their creation from less-fluid lava flows that were then more prone to weathering. That the earthworks provided inspiration for the formal naming of both a town and an iconic rock offers evidence that the landscape has moved others besides me.

The change from the region's more common basalt, organized in tight, impenetrable layers, also provides something of practical value. A pair of ravines, located on a fault line separating two different rhyolite flows, intersect the canyon across from each to other provide a near perfect crossing. The passage represents a stark contrast to Lilly Grade, which had to be hacked out of one side of the canyon before making a twisted exit from the other. The vehicles that zoom by as I walk the road make it down and up in a couple of minutes. I wave at two separate ranchers who I know as they head into the desert, but neither recognizes the bundled pedestrian out in the raw, blustery weather.

The openings through the fortress of rhyolite towers served as a travel corridor long before motorists, hikers, or any white people considered calling this region home. Native Americans were the first humans to wear a path down into the canyon. The access provided them with a means to not only reach the opposite side, but also utilize food resources inside the gorge itself. In addition to valuable plants, small game, and birds held within the landscape's crease, the stream offered salmon and steelhead pushing their way upstream.

Kelly Murphey, a longtime resident and local prehistory authority, tells me that the "Ancient Ones" did not live here year-round but utilized the canyon's shelter and harvested its protein as part of their seasonal rounds. Over the course of the year the aboriginal people, usually living together as family unit, might travel from the Snake River in the spring to the Nevada highlands in the summer. Their route remained near the canyon, but usually not for what it contained within its depths. While those staples were accessible at the crossing near Balanced Rock, too much energy was expended elsewhere descending into the deep, rough canyon. The reward was simply not worth the effort. The real value in traveling along the rim came when hunters pursued prey. The horseless natives used its abrupt edge to improve their chance of a kill, if they had a big enough group of people, by controlling their prey's movement and preventing easy escape.

Without a doubt the convenient stretch of canyon at Balanced Rock served as a popular spot for the region's native inhabitants. Remnants of a salmon fishing weir and a basket trap made of willows were found early in the last century. In the 1950s during the construction of a county park, a cache of over two-dozen projectile points, commonly referred to as arrowheads, were unearthed. A separate discovery from a nearby rock shelter in the vicinity included items vital to subsistence like a bone hide scraper, numerous snares and pieces of a trapping kit, and six feet of braided sage bark. A comb and a ball composed of deer hide stuffed with moss were also included in the mix. Kelly, whose passion for archaeology led to his obtaining a master's degree and spending many summers in the field while pursuing a career in education, says that those findings were likely a few thousand years old.

The deadfall trapping kit, utilizing sticks to prop up a rock until a rodent finds its way underneath, helps tell the story of a division of labor between genders. Kelly notes that the trap lines were often patrolled by women in an effort to help supplement the salmon fishing. Women probably contributed more to the nutritional needs of their group by collecting plants, seeds, insects, and small fish or animals. If something could be speared or shot with a bow and arrow, the men were then likely to participate. The amount of socializing done in the hunter-gatherer groups spoke to their overall productivity. Kelly says that they undoubtedly had times when things went poorly and there were leaner seasons of subsistence, but in a typical year they were able to garner enough from their focused efforts to be able to enjoy life.

As a boy I also heard several stories, their specifics now forgotten, from my father and other locals of artifacts being found in the canyon. With those distant narratives and more recently Kelly's insight, any entrance now into the park at Balanced Rock leaves me feeling there is more to this landscape than the sum of the rocks and plants and water and sky. It takes little effort to imagine that others were present long before people of my skin color came onto the scene. On this January day that I stroll upstream through the silent chasm, protected from the wind, the only sounds made are those of my boots scuffing across the asphalt. As their echo bounces off the rock walls, I wonder about other human noises the canyon once hosted.

Before long I hear something not of any person's creation. What sounds like the occasional chirp from a bird draws my gaze into the cliffs above me. Expecting to find something of a feathered nature, I see nothing at first, but then am surprised to spy a yellow-bellied marmot. Known locally as a rock chuck, the critter is tucked back into a recess thirty feet above the ground where two pillars pull away from each other. Two hundred years earlier natives would have looked at him as dinner. My perspective as a farmer would have seen him as a pest. On this day, however, he simply appears as an animal engaging with his outside world after a five-month hibernation. A marmot's heart rate during their deep sleep drops from a normal rate of ninety beats per minute to only four. Their internal body temperature levels off to a few degrees above that of their winter burrow—as low as thirty-eight degrees Fahrenheit. Those adaptations, which allow the animal to live off fat reserves, seem hard to fathom.

As I observe the rodent, the first of the species seen this year, I think about his autumn and winter existence. I also seem unable to resist applying human emotions to the animal and its present state of being. The chirping and tail twitching seem to indicate some form of turmoil. Perhaps he might be grumpy after such a long nap or just happy to be seeing the outside world again—and willing to tell anything or anybody about it. I consider that he might be upset about my presence, but realize I heard the chirps before arriving here. I then chide myself for being so anthropomorphic after recalling that after waking in the spring the dominant male will drive other males away from his harem. The whole show might be only about sex.

The rock chuck's ruckus fades behind me as I walk upstream through the park. The narrow strip of floodplain between the creek and the foot of the cliffs is a popular place to escape spring winds and come for the year's first picnic. In addition, the towering canyon walls provide ample shelter from the scorching sun during the summer. Deserted in the winter, however, it makes for a perfect spot to take a solitary stroll.

The landscape's charm becomes more calming as I allow myself to slow down and look around. Not all the rhyolite comes in the form of towering vertical cliffs—many rock figures, called hoodoos, morph into a variety of creatures, real and make-believe. I spy the profile of an American president across the creek, an elephant's head at the next bend, a goblin lurking above. The experience feels like that of a younger me lying on my back and appraising a sky filled with floating clouds. The shapes that now appear and vanish, however, only result when the movement is mine. The magic again brings the Ancient Ones to the forefront of my consciousness. What did they see in the stone, and how did those images fit into their stories? Lured here by shelter, protein, and other life necessities, how could they not forget about the tasks at hand and look up and dream?

A quarter mile upstream from the road crossing, a path begins where the park ends. The trail is easily the most traveled in the entire canyon, offering explorers more views of stone sculptures. The stretch of creek also serves as the easiest place to paddle a canoe or kayak since no boulders or rapids interrupt the lazy nature of its flow. Meandering along the path, I am reminded of the surprising amount of color the canyon offers even in the dead of winter. Willow thickets crowd the creek with bare red stems that reach twice my height. Last year's growth of tall reed grass, cured tan, mingle with the outside edge of the willows. Even those rocks without interesting shapes contribute to the pleasing scene with a rust-colored base speckled with yellow and green lichen. At certain vantage points the glassy surface of the stream reflects all those objects along with a ribbon of sky bluer than when observed directly.

The tranquil atmosphere is interrupted when the canyon tests my nerve as I encounter a cliff that plunges down to the creek before sloping outward several feet to meet the water. I remove my gloves, stash them in my pack, and edge around the rock. The rhyolite's pitted surface offers numerous handholds and traction for my feet near the water's surface. My slow movement is composed of a four-beat rhythm as my left hand and then foot reach out first and are then followed by their counterparts. The cliff crossing lasts less than a minute, but I come away surprised at how quickly the rock transfers its cold to my fingers.

Beyond that obstacle the creek harbors waterfowl. I jump a pair of mallards followed by three more. Around the next bend an integrated flock of ten ducks, both mallards and teal, spring from the water. In some places the dense strip of willows serves as a screen between me and the floating birds. When one flock flushes beside me unseen until they climb into the sky, I am not sure who is more surprised. Around the next bend I spot another bunch loitering along a stretch devoid of much cover. Inspired by the ghosts of past hunters and gatherers, my own instincts, and the presence of prey, I hunker down into stalk mode. After crawling on all fours for a few minutes, a peek through the sagebrush enables me to get a fix on their position. I feel deserving of a pat on the back having crept within fifty feet of them. Their tight cluster and unease tell me that they sense my presence but cannot confirm it. The birds hold steady.

That my stealth has little to do with sneaking close to the ducks becomes obvious when I glance up. The predator that has drawn their attention comes in the form of a fellow bird soaring a couple hundred yards away near the canyon rim. The golden eagle makes several graceful circles as it rides the ceaseless wind that has been mostly forgotten about down here. I feel a little foolish—while focusing on the ducks I nearly missed spotting the majestic bird. To add insult to injury, my binoculars remain stuffed inside my daypack. I retrieve the optics and search for the eagle, but the bird of prey has likely spotted me and banks out of sight around the next bend.

As I move again upstream, the forgotten ducks feel safe enough to flush and escape in the other direction. The loud whoosh of the group takeoff startles me. After being thoroughly humbled by nature in a matter of minutes, I collect myself and continue the hike upstream.

I soon arrive at a spot where two large boulders protrude from the creek and clutch a large tree trunk. The remains of the gnarled juniper were first encountered twenty years ago during my initial canoe trip upstream from the park. At that time I perceived it and the rocks as obstacles that forced me to abandon the water and drag the canoe around them. With successive paddle trips over the last few years, however, I have become more appreciative of the chunk of wood. The juniper's four-foot-diameter base is about as big as I have observed for that species, but in less than twenty feet the tree spirals down to a six-inch top where it had been sawed off. The bottom of the trunk shows no sign of human markings, however, and its root remnants indicate that the goliath was ripped from the earth by an impressive force.

While I suspect that the removal occurred during an emergency release of water at Salmon Dam in 1984 that caused a devastating flood, there is no way to confirm my hunch. The tree possesses a story, including a chapter about human alteration, but I know nothing except that it has long remained firmly wedged between those boulders. Resting with feet on wood and backside to rock, I ponder the juniper's displacement, downstream journey, and present resting place. Another entry is placed in my mind's ledger of the mysteries held inside this canyon.

The gorge twists to the left and leads to a stretch of creek containing several clusters of boulders and fast water that put an end to most upstream paddling. I cling to a vague recollection of having been this far on foot once in pursuit of ducks with my father. As my thoughts slip back and I try to remember something about the trip, my legs keep propelling me forward until I face another cliff that drops into the creek. At twenty feet high the obstacle is not nearly as tall as the one encountered earlier, but its vertical profile means there will be no edging around its base. I see a couple of seams in the adjoining cluster of rocks where it appears possible to climb upward. I again search for a memory from four decades ago but fail.

My mind begins to cloud with doubts about whether Dad and I came this far, or if we did, other challenges that might lurk around the next corner. I even second-guess myself about us being on this side of the creek. In turn my diminishing confidence seems to affect all else. After spending too much time weighing my ability to climb, I make a couple of tentative attempts to clamber up through one of the folds in the outcrop. Feeling every bit of my fifty-four years and one day on this earth, I return to the ground and elect to turn back. I remind myself that the original plan called for climbing out of the canyon and looping back to Balanced Rock along the rim. It seems the time to do that has arrived, but the reversal in direction is accompanied by the twinge of defeat.

I backtrack a quarter mile and scan my side of the canyon. A break in the rhyolite walls along the creek offers an opportunity to ascend. The upper cliffs and talus prompt some anxiety as I weave upward, but the obstacles are not of the caliber that thwarted me earlier. After reaching the top I duck back down when greeted by the full force of the wind. A hospitable boulder offers protection from the biting gusts while also allowing me to bask in full sunlight.

With my back to the rock I eat lunch, look back down into the canyon, and review the spot that turned me back. As I ponder the rock face from a distance, a memory of an outing assigned to another place breaks free from my subconscious—and my mind is infused with a boost of clarity. It was at the foot of this cliff, seen now, that my father and I stood and discussed strategy. He then wedged his body into and up the three-sided chimney. After he found secure footing, we leaned toward each other and stretched our arms just far enough for me to hand him, one at a time, our unloaded shotguns. Then my turn came to climb up through the chute.

My young Labrador retriever presented us with the biggest issue. We needed to get Sue around the obstacle too, but she would have nothing to do with being hoisted up to where she might claw the remaining pitch to my father. I could not fault her reluctance. After Dad and I made it to the top of the outcrop, and safely back down to the creek, we were forced into hoping that she would jump in and swim around the cliff. While only separated by thirty feet, however, the cliff's bulge prevented us and Sue from seeing each other. We pleaded softly and she whined. We yelled encouragement and she barked. We said nothing and received silence in return. At one point we caught a glimpse of her trotting back down the trail at the next bend, but thankfully she responded to our panicked cries and returned.

Eventually my dog overcame her fear, slipped into the water, and paddled around the cliff. After our happy reunion consisting of an intense period of praise and tail-wagging, we hunted upstream a bit more. Our return journey required that we repeat some of the theatrics to again entice her around the cliff. No wonder we three only made that trip once.

That this memory tucked away and attributed to a different location in the canyon could be plucked out and properly sorted feels amazing. Apparently it had taken a step back—or in this case several hundred—from the cliff in order to get an objective view of time and place. I am not sure what to make of the incident other than to confirm that memory can be suspect—and to know enough to thank the landscape for providing another gift.

Feeling ready to take on the incessant wind, I pop back up to the edge of the plain. After getting a look at the surrounding terrain, I confirm that today's trek has nearly intersected with my journey from earlier in the month. I judge that to be close enough, and make a hard right-hand turn and head back downstream. With the crumbled rim having all but disappeared, the crowns of those stone towers that I passed underneath a few hours ago draw my interest. I angle back down a bit and explore the tops of the rock formations that spring from the bottom of the canyon. An attempt to parallel the creek from my lofty perspective becomes impossible when several small ravines that dive into the canyon force me into a clockwise contour around them.

After surprising a few mule deer tucked away in the rolling landscape and watching them bound away into the next fold, I make one more meander back to the canyon. A scramble to the crown of one tower provides both a panorama of the Salmon Falls Creek drainage and the opposing gullies that carry the road crossing. In addition, I receive a bird's-eye view of the park directly below. The landscape holds not only the present intersection of creek and pavement, but also the existence of different people and eras. On the final half mile back to the morning's departure point, I cannot help but feel that the multidimensional web has also entwined me.

Chapter 3

FEBRUARY 8

Snubbed twice the previous month, Balanced Rock gains my full attention in February. Before hiking up to the main attraction, I cross the road to look at an interpretative sign that reads like a prize-fighter's tale of the tape. At forty-eight feet high by forty feet wide, the rock's dimensions are especially striking when compared to how little support its thin base provides—only three feet by seventeen and a half inches. The final item of the brief description then offers a hint as to its creation: "A rhyolite monolith shaped by differential weathering." But the words and numbers alone do not account for the full wonder. How does this chunk of stone, its question-mark shape providing an element of grace, continue to stand? The sight almost defies reason.

And while the view from the road is rewarding, getting the best feel for this iconic fixture requires a closer perspective. After glancing back and forth from sign to rock a few times, I step back across the pavement and skid down a small gulley. Taking baby steps to avoid slipping, I then ascend the steep hillside on a worn but snow-covered path. It's not just the slope that works against me—the white stuff underfoot has become such a rare commodity that I am not accustomed to walking on it. Half of the five inches that fell yesterday melted overnight, but the remainder still amounts to the most that a single storm has gifted our area this winter. And I am not the only one enjoying the novelty. On my drive this morning I passed several snowmen standing in the front yards of rural homes.

Even with the slick incline the hike from the parking lot to Balanced Rock takes less than five minutes. The climb is punctuated with brief pauses that allow me to shift the focus from my feet to the monument. Having seen the local attraction dozens of times, I still cannot keep from looking upward. With this morning's thoughts drifting toward how long that slim column can support a mass weighing forty tons, I speculate on the day the landmark tumbles down. The stem will eventually erode and weaken to a point where something gives way. Will it crack under the pressure and allow the rock to simply drop, or will a fateful event like a violent wind gust or tremor from inside the earth elbow it into unbalance?

Hopefully people will not have a hand in its demise, but who knows? Early in the previous century various residents used horses and ropes, dynamite, and even hand tools in hopes of felling the rock. The common excuse to topple it seemed most often based on safety concerns since the road once ran closer to the formation, but I wonder. Perhaps part of humanity is simply prone to mischief or the inability to leave things as they are. The fact that at least one attempt was made to apply concrete to the base, however, hints at the protective side of mankind.

As I continue my ascent and consider the how and when of Balanced Rock's fall, it occurs to me that my paltry body walks in the path of the massive stone once it does drop and roll. I count on nothing happening in the next few moments, but my pace quickens.

Conjecture about the rock's future disappears when I discover spray paint on its foundation and several companion pillars. Part of me is prompted to wish that the landmark be hidden away from the road where its chances of remaining untouched are better. On the other hand, I am grateful that so many people can visit and have the chance to exclaim, "Wow, look at that!" And I do know that the act of leaving one's mark is not a recent phenomenon; newspaper accounts indicate that people have been "autographing" the local anomaly for a long time. Prior to that, even Native Americans sometimes etched or painted on rocks, although no evidence has been found locally. Perhaps I should not judge and give the artwork that I have seen of native people a significantly higher value than the present entries, but in the end my attempt at open-mindedness loses out. It just seems like little more than graffiti. Is it too much to ask that nature's stonework be left alone?

I leave the blemished rock face behind and am greeted by tiny streams of water running down a stone shelf that tilts to my feet. Some of the liquid comes from Balanced Rock itself. The melting snow on top first creeps down its sides but then loses grip where the profile begins to pinch inward. When I look up the rock rains on my face, but the cold moisture is allowed to run down the curve of my own head and neck. The shower seems to help wash off some of the irritation still stuck to me after discovering the paint. The spot beneath the rock also provides refuge to watch and listen to the water's movement while inhaling the musky air. After my hand runs along the rough surface of the rhyolite, a closer inspection reveals the stone's grainy, erosive texture. The contact serves as a reminder of how easy it is to miss the individual pieces of a thing while trying to take in its entirety.

After my pause underneath Balanced Rock, I scramble up several more slabs of wet stone and reach a vantage point not quite a hundred feet beyond the landmark. The spot puts me nearly at eye level with the top of the stone and provides an ideal position from where to photograph its silhouette. I most often arrive near sundown and hope for a background sky that harbors a few clouds that might blossom into a palette of colors. The best opportunity comes near the winter solstice, when the sun sets at its farthest point south. Usually nothing much happens except for me becoming chilled, but when everything comes together the visual transcends the cold. On this overcast morning, however, the flat light offers little to work with. The camera stays in my pack and I walk away. Exploring sounds like a more rewarding option.

I gain more elevation and then wander along the tops of other towers that stand in a slightly curved line near the road as it drops into the canyon. That same process responsible for shaping the area's most popular resident also deserves credit for the creation of most all the rockwork in the vicinity—including those profiles that mesmerized me during last week's meander through the park. To understand how all this came to be, I consulted with Shawn Willsey, a geology professor at the College of Southern Idaho. He has enlightened me numerous times about the region's landscapes and possesses that knack for summarizing an idea with just enough terminology to make you feel enlightened, rather than dizzy.

Before we delved into the actual sculpting process, Shawn wanted me to first understand why the erosive rhyolite was present. I had seen plenty of the neatly layered, gray basalt upstream—why did this random jumble of brown rock show up here? He pointed out that in the middle of the Snake River Plain, rhyolite is almost always older and therefore lies underneath the stacks of basalt. With the Balanced Rock area being far enough away from that central zone, however, the basalt flows here sometimes ended up being not as thick. In addition, he asked me to visualize the underlying rhyolite as not being a horizontal, level surface. In this location that lava production left a high point. The subsequent, thinner basalt flows then could only lap around the edges of that elevated terrain.

When trying to grasp the meaning of differential weathering, I knew that I was talking to the right person—Shawn provided the narrative for the sign down near the parking lot. The process is dependent on several factors. Due to the varied composition of the rock and its hardness, the material will weather and erode at different rates. Moisture will repeatedly move into the rock's fractures, freeze, and eventually split it along these weak zones. Over the eons, and still happening now, the freeze-thaw cycles break some of the stone apart and leave the more resilient outcrops isolated.

Yesterday's snowfall has transformed the bench and its formations above Balanced Rock into an even more appealing place than usual. From one perspective the white ground cover serves as the perfect contrast for the bare brown rock of the hoodoos. On their windward faces, however, the surfaces soften and outlines blur where the snow still sticks like a coat of paint. In addition to absorbing the dynamic scene that I walk through, my gaze periodically drops down in case the blanket of snow might reveal signs of wildlife.

I soon cut a coyote's track and follow its trail toward a cluster of low rhyolite outcrops. In one spot the predator hopped up on one that offered a good vantage point before jumping back down to continue its search. The prints lead me through a labyrinth of stone formations before heading back onto the open hillside. Where they briefly mix with another set of canine tracks before each diverge in separate directions, I split the difference and again wander through untracked snow.

A solitary chukar partridge flushes from a protected spot underneath the lip of a boulder. The game bird zips over the rocks and out of sight in a matter of seconds, giving me no time to apologize for my intrusion. Soon after that brief encounter, I spy a much larger bird perched on the cross arm of a power pole standing near the rim of the Salmon Falls canyon. The golden eagle allows me to approach close enough to discern his plumage rustling in the wind. When I consider taking a better look through binoculars, I realize that they are still lying on the kitchen table. I scold myself for having spoiled opportunities for a close-up view of the species twice in two weeks—and likely of the same bird or its mate.

The eagle initially shows little concern as I attempt to angle away from its overlook, but after a few minutes it tires of my presence. The majestic predator crouches and springs from the wood perch, unfolds its wings, and disappears down into the gorge. I scan the horizon above the canyon in both directions in hopes of another glimpse, but the void appears to have swallowed the bird up.

I reach the point on the rim that allows me to peer down at both Salmon Falls Creek and the deep ravine that cradles the road. The view is superb, but not a surprise—near the end of my last outing I stood only a quarter mile away on the other side of the pavement. The park again looks deserted, although two sets of tracks drawn through the snow, likely from the same vehicle entering and leaving, indicate some level of interest.

As I move downstream along the rim, the rhyolite columns underfoot mark some of the tallest and most precarious that I have encountered in the entire area. The caps of several pillars tempt me to edge out farther for a peek straight down, but few of them look safely negotiable with their glaze of snow. Reluctant to withdraw, I search for a suitable route that might lead to a perch. An occasional opening between the stone towers teases me with a glimpse of the canyon floor and creek, but after ten minutes of probing and a few slips in the slush, I scramble back to safer ground.

A few minutes later the sight of steel pipes seizes my attention. Up to two feet in diameter, they rise along the steep hillside before slipping through a break in the cliffs. The pipelines originate from a series of pumps that suck water from the creek during the farming season and push the prized liquid up and out of the canyon. This and other pumping stations downstream supply irrigation water to a tract of isolated farmland on the desert side of the canyon called Magic Water. The source is a combination of the leakage around Salmon Dam, natural springs, and both surface and ground water coming from the irrigation of farmland to the east. Specific amounts as determined by a legal water right are withdrawn by farmers, ensuring that some water remains year-round in the creek channel. The flow has varied significantly only once, when the 1984 emergency spill at Salmon Dam swept through the canyon. When the floodwater temporarily pooled up behind the road crossing and then tore through its earthen fill, the deluge destroyed the pumping station below me.

I leave the canyon's notched rim and follow the set of pipelines up a gradual incline. My interest in irrigation as an ex-farmer and through my current job with the Natural Resources Conservation Service causes me to linger when I find that two of the pipes end before reaching any sort of destination. The other two conduits, also the largest, show no similar signs of abandonment when I discover that they end at the head of two conveyance ditches. In a few months water lifted from the creek will be dropped into them and be transported across the contour of the slope. On this day, however, the laterals contain little but tumbleweeds partially covered by drifted snow.

My next destination becomes the top of the small butte that I have already begun to ascend. The rise will provide me with another prime vantage point during my hike back to Balanced Rock along a different route. Fifteen minutes later I stand on top but am rewarded with limited visibility due to low clouds that now promise rain. While the partial view of farmland in one direction and rangeland in the other is striking, it's still the meandering split in the earth separating them that holds my focus.

The scene prompts me to consider how little I know of this drainage. Sure, I have inspected a map countless times and traced the canyon's path as it slices from one end of the county to the other. But of the thirty miles that served as a channel for that spill water to race from Salmon Dam to this crossing, I have seen, until a month ago, little more than a half dozen. The twenty-mile section that funneled the torrent from here to the Snake River is even less familiar.

The self-interrogation begins after acknowledging that those unfamiliar stretches of Salmon Falls Creek likely offer a variety of rewarding scenes and encounters. What have I been doing? What am I waiting for? Lack of access or opportunity is not the culprit—few spots along the canyon amount to more than an hour's drive from home. I can no longer blame our family farm. During the past ten years I have worked a conventional schedule, so the excuse of insufficient time no longer has merit. Other than an occasional sore hip, my body seems reasonably fit and mobile. I confirmed that last month when my feet and legs propelled me farther than they ever had in a single day.

As I sit on a small boulder, look at the canyon, and examine my excuses, an idea starts to coalesce that before has only taken the form of random bursts of interest. What about walking the length of the canyon along the rim, in bits and pieces, from its mouth to the dam? Each section of unknown country could be examined like a puzzle piece and placed into position. If those journeys went well, I could hike along the dozen miles of pooled water behind the dam. I might then even take on the remote section from the reservoir's backwaters to the state boundary.

My mind meanders up the drainage but soon shifts gears. Why stop at the border? Why not plunge into Nevada, explore entirely unfamiliar country, and then climb into the mountains that harbor the creek's source? Why not turn the journey into a yearlong endeavor by tackling each portion as work and weather permits?

No arguments come up to slow down my racing mind, but with this fresh mindset I likely would not entertain them if they did. Even my ongoing dilemma about visiting old versus new landscapes suddenly seems to carry little weight. Returning to a familiar spot, of course, has its appeal. I know where wildlife can be found or what inspiring landscape feature lies around the next bend in the creek, trail, or road. Visiting such a place is often as comforting as meeting up with friends or family. The present can be embraced, previous experiences relived, and future get-togethers planned. It's easy going back to a piece of land that I know will not let me down. Salmon Falls Creek certainly passes through a few miles of country that keep beckoning for my return.

I see more clearly, however, that loyalty has its drawbacks. Devotion to a few choice environments prevents me from finding others, exploring them, and forming new connections. And as the familiar becomes safe, the element of surprise goes away. Traversing a piece of ground for the first time also brings with it freedom—there is not yet a standard route or special spot that might control the experience. A journey through the unknown requires a leap of faith. Will my chosen course take me from start to finish, and if so, do I possess both the resolve and the ability to make it there? The next question addresses my own mortality. How much time before I physically cannot take on this type of hiking project, or worse, just give up on the idea?

At some point on my loop back to Balanced Rock, I pass the threshold where consideration of the adventure evolves into anticipation. Part of me wants to jump right into some serious planning, but I tell myself to wait and just enjoy this day. Soon after I accept that advice, a breeze picks up and brings a splatter of rain that again seems directed at my face. Out of habit I pull my hood up, but then let its protection fall back down. There is no way a light shower can dampen my spirit, and with precipitation of any sort meager this past year, it almost feels impolite to not be fully welcoming. If this weather and land can find a way to seep into me, I will surely accept their gift.

Chapter 4

FEBRUARY 23

The notion to explore the Salmon Falls Creek drainage comes much easier than the plan. The first issue involves sorting out where and how to begin. During the brainstorm at Balanced Rock, I conveniently ignored the creek's last few non-canyon miles that meander through private property. A smattering of residential homes standing near the stream's banks makes foot travel impossible. Highway 30 crosses the creek and is rarely more than a quarter mile away before it enters the Snake River, but I balk at that route. Walking along pavement next to noisy, speeding traffic seems like a poor way to begin a promising adventure.

After considering the dilemma for several weeks and talking to a few locals, I conclude that the creek itself is the solution. A float trip from the highway bridge down to the river appears to be the best option. The mode and direction of travel differ from my original idea, but I remind myself that no firm guidance exists. The only condition that I envisioned was that the journey be completed with feet and legs. If that self-propelled form of transportation needs to be expanded to some arm power, so be it.

While I do not possess more than a chunky seventeen-foot canoe and a minimal amount of ability, I am lucky enough to have a willing partner: my wife. Recently retired from a career focused on helping others, particularly at-risk teenagers, she now has the time and energy for some new experiences. After listening to my original idea that consisted of a series of hikes, Beth wanted to accompany me on a few. Her interest did not waver even after hearing that the first outing consisted of a float trip.

The last Sunday in February brings with it favorable weather to canoe the creek. The forecast calls for a clear, calm day with temperatures bumping sixty degrees for the first time since last autumn. After driving a half hour from our home, Beth and I pull off the highway and into the parking lot at Miracle Hot Springs, one of several family-owned resorts fed by springwater on the south side of the Snake River. An overnight camper notices our arrival and visits with us as we unload the canoe and prepare to launch. Right before we push off he cautions us about a couple of distant obstacles—a fence and pipeline—that cross the stream.

The canoe is hardly wet, however, before we run into our first challenge. After passing underneath the highway bridge, we encounter a tree hanging over a short stretch of water that bobs through a cluster of boulders. The combination serves as a reminder that it has been a while since Beth and I have shared a canoe together. The price to pay for our clumsy passage is extracted by a tree limb that scrapes skin from my nose and several knuckles. I am relieved that we remain afloat, but the brief test does nothing to bolster my confidence about our expedition. An ideal outing during one of our occasional canoe trips consists of paddling across a serene, unobstructed surface. We lack the skill or desire to take on much more. What else lurks downstream between us and the river?

We soon find out. After a stretch of calm water allows us to loosen up and work a bit on technique, we approach a submerged shelf of rocks lying at the head of another short rapid. Unable to see much, we make a timid approach toward the center of the creek and grind to a stop across the top of a hidden boulder. Our old canoe then spins ninety degrees to the east like a compass needle before lodging on both the initial rock and its partner. Remaining stuck does not seem like such a bad alternative, however, when faced with the prospect of the canoe slipping off the snag and dumping us broadside into the laughing rapids below. I envision a boatful of cold water and a panicked scramble to shore. A shiver sweeps over me when I realize that we possess little in the way of spare dry clothes in case of a dunking.

After a terse debate on how to escape our predicament, we twitch our bodies several times in unison. Our actions resemble an awkward herky-jerky dance move, but we manage to inch the canoe closer to the bank. Beth then grabs our towrope made of baling twine—even as ex-farmers we still have a handy supply—and jumps to dry land. I immediately follow her lead and abandon ship. With the canoe now only holding food, drinking water, and our cameras stuffed in a dry bag, it floats off the rocks and swings back to the bank.

Safe for the time being, I again wonder what else Salmon Falls Creek has in store for us. I also begin to question my scheme, although not out loud. Our dubious skill level would only be frustrating had it not also created a threat to our well-being. The distasteful option of walking along the highway and sharing that route with motor vehicles now sounds more tolerable, but we are long past the point of a do-over. We have committed to paddling this canoe to the end of the creek and beyond.

Most of the stream's remaining course mercifully provides us with tame water and the chance to enjoy our surroundings and the wildlife it harbors. On one stretch willow thickets border the stream on both sides to form a tunnel-like passage. In less confined spaces mallards launch from the creek, chastising us for our trespass into their haven. As the canoe slips around one tight bend we surprise a pair of geese that offer their own theatrical response as they flee. Quail flush from the bank's shrubbery, and on one occasion we spot a muskrat racing downstream. Even on portions of the creek that require active paddling, Beth and I settle into a quiet, smooth glide.

Halfway to the river we encounter a spot where the flow drops several feet over a rock ledge. After portaging around the hazard and again embarking, I glance back at the arc of water plunging over and down. Two words came to mind: *Salmon. Falls.* Though the creek's name is derived from a feature several miles below its mouth on the Snake River, those two words also seem tied to this spot. The cascade might bear little resemblance, since much of the area has seen man's imprint, to what it did when the iconic fish swam here. I have little trouble, however, visualizing a finned creature leaping from the water, stretching upward to the next tier, and pushing on to its birthplace.

Along the way we duck underneath not only the pipeline and fence that we were warned about, but also a low concrete bridge. After running one final short stretch of rough water without smacking into any more rocks, I offer a subdued cheer. Beth counters that perhaps our success likely has more to do with luck than skill. She might be correct, but my relief is still fused with triumph.

We then let the canoe drift until the creek comes to a near standstill and splits into a pair of corridors that offer passage around either side of a small river island. Eager to enter open water, we steer into the one that appears to offer the shortest access. Within fifty yards the canoe bottoms out on sediment dropped in the transition zone between our creek and the Snake River. This time we welcome the halt of progress. Basking under the warming sun seems like a fine way to spend a few minutes. We let go of our paddles, held earlier at times in what seemed like a death grip, and enjoy the chance to absorb surroundings that are not constantly on the move.

This spot where water blends from as far away as two other states, Wyoming and Nevada, once served as the last noteworthy exit from the Snake River for historic salmon and steelhead returning to their birthplace. Fish could still move upriver, but only for another thirty miles until the 212-foot-tall Shoshone Falls emphatically blocked all traffic. While the number of fish and how far they progressed up Salmon Falls Creek remains a mystery, evidence indicates that some might have pushed into Nevada.

By the end of the nineteenth century, the size of most anadromous runs in the Pacific Northwest had started shrinking due to habitat loss and commercial overfishing after the arrival of white Euro-Americans. A hydroelectric dam constructed in 1903 on the Snake River downstream then effectively served as the death knell for salmon and steelhead populations. While that structure at Swan Falls thirty miles southwest of Boise was constructed with fish ladders, the capability to pass up- or downstream was severely restricted. Idaho Power modified their ladder system in 1922, but little improvement occurred. When the C. J. Strike Dam between Swan Falls and Salmon Falls Creek was built thirty years later, the design did not even bother to address fish passage. With the taming of the Snake River for hydroelectric and irrigation purposes nearly complete, the migratory fish were locked out of southern Idaho.

Long ago when I worked on a grade school project about salmon, I possessed little knowledge about the significance of a natural barrier like the "Niagara of the West" or those first man-made constructions. I do recall my artwork depicting a mountain range on one side of a three-foot-wide sheet of paper and the ocean on its opposite edge. Underneath the ribbon of blue that linked those two features I placed the focal point—a single fish that exhibited some of the sparkling colors that I had seen in a hardbound encyclopedia. I hold no memory of the species and if the Snake River even flowed in the right direction on my map. Despite having resided in a landlocked state my entire life, however, I still retain a fascination about the life cycle and instinct that guides young fish downstream and the imprint that later pulls them back up as adults. Some of nature's most compelling stories no doubt include the one of fish that ends with a return to their birthplace and an offer of new life just before their own death.

Prior to the hazards of commercial fishing in the late nineteenth century and then the building of dams, some fish still did not complete their last chapter once they left the river. After making a right-hand turn from where Beth and I now linger, the first few miles of Salmon Falls Creek proved perilous to salmon and steelhead. Native Americans who wintered in a village near the mouth of the creek usually stayed into the spring to harvest fish before most of them made their own journey toward higher elevations. The area along the stretch we just floated also became a popular spot for Oregon Trail emigrants passing through southern Idaho in August. The camp was a welcome respite for pioneers plodding through the sweltering desert and for many travelers offered the first dependable water in several days. Diary entries also mentioned salmon fishing and enjoying a fresh alternative to their normal diet.

After finishing our break we stash our food and gear back into their bag and prepare to move on. Our float trip cannot end here at the mouth of Salmon Falls Creek—no access to a public road and a waiting vehicle exists. But we would not stop even if the means to return home were handy. Only five miles separate us from this spot where the creek's physical identity ends and the place where its name originated. A voyage down the river will nearly connect those two points.

We back the canoe out from the shallow water covering the mudflat and then paddle out into the Snake River. Our graduation from the creek's maximum thirty-foot width to an expanse of water several hundred yards across energizes us. The creek had started to become a little confining, and while it did allow us an occasional sideways glance, our concern remained on the potential perils directly ahead. On the river we can readjust our focus to more distant sights and in any direction we choose.

Much of the pleasing scenery comes in the form of springwater entering our new environment. Two notable sources, unseen around the next bend upstream, briefly tempt us into taking a two-mile round-trip detour. Blueheart Springs is blessed with water that bubbles up into an alcove along the Snake, offering the clearest pool that I have ever seen. A short distance from there, North America's eleventh-largest spring enters the river after boiling up from the head of a deep gorge called Box Canyon that runs little more than a mile in length. We agree to stick to our plans, however, and angle slightly downstream toward the middle of the river.

Feeling the need to slow down after having encountered more than expected during our busy morning, we cease paddling. The canoe, aligned with an infrequent stroke, drifts with the faint current toward flotillas of migratory waterfowl still clinging to their winter range. A mix of wing beats, quacks, and honks from several species of ducks and Canada geese produce a frenzied clamor. Hundreds of birds, maybe a thousand, lift from the water in waves and organize into squadrons that seem to briefly patrol the sky before circling and heading upriver. Dark gray coots attempting their own escape make us smile as their frenzied mix of flapping and running lifts them only a few feet above the water's surface. Their short flights end quickly after moving a safe distance downstream, but require repetition when we again approach too close.

Beth and I cross over toward the river's east bank not only to escape the noise of the highway, but also to get closer to the region's most obvious swarm of springs. Even before this stretch became known as Thousand Springs, the area drew high praise. Journal entries from pioneers heading to Oregon gushed over the spectacle of water flowing from the side of the canyon. Prior to those visitors, many of the first white explorers took note. When John C. Frémont passed through the Hagerman Valley in 1843 during an expedition in search of a route to the Pacific, he wrote about the scene in his journal: "Over the edge of the black cliffs and out of their faces, are falling numberless streams and springs."

The water's source is an aquifer underlying the eastern Snake River Plain that is often called southern Idaho's most valuable resource. Besides its importance to farms and fish hatcheries, the pristine liquid serves as the sole source of drinking water for three hundred thousand people. While most often compared to Lake Erie in size, calling the water body an underground lake might be simplistic. Many experts refer to it as something more like a sponge that has a network of pores that allows water to seep in a lateral fashion rather than be held in a static state. Fed by irrigation, rain and snowmelt, and other surface and underground sources, the conduit of fractured basalt allows passage toward the southwest from as far away as the Wyoming border.

The liquid moves in super slow-motion; two hundred years might pass before a drop of water travels from one end of the aquifer to the other. Most of it stays within several hundred feet of the surface, and where the Snake River Canyon has cut down and intersected those lava flows, the lifeblood escapes. A thirty-mile section of the canyon receives the bulk of the water released at the tail end of the aquifer. Beth and I are now fortunate enough to float next to the largest concentration of those outlets.

We abandon the river after a mile and point our canoe into one of those spring-fed tributaries. Paddling our bulky craft against the strong current requires all the resolve we can muster. The flow comes from a multitude of sources, some that possess enough volume and elevation above the river that they are first diverted to spin electricity-producing turbines. The water eventually enters the river from different directions and isolates a lowland area known as Ritter Island. The land once served as the site of a small dairy operation originating in the 1920s that consisted of a premium herd of Guernsey cows. The island's history and scenery are now highlighted by the Idaho Department of Parks and Recreation, but that agency first needed a willing partner. The Nature Conservancy served that role by purchasing the property, making improvements, and later donating it to the state. The site also hosts an annual festival that draws talented artists and thousands of visitors during a single weekend in September.

On our outing, however, we observe only a handful of visitors: a pair of kayakers and two couples hiking on either side of the main stream. Beth and I escape the canoe for the first time since our float trip began and walk over to admire the largest waterfall in the area. The most visible from the highway across the river, the cascade becomes less of a scene and more of an experience when standing close enough for the mist to gently brush our faces. We linger at the waterfall, savoring its shower down, over, and into the rocks. The water's rumble blocks out all other sounds, but even if we could hear each other, we likely would not speak.

On the return trip down the short stream, we place our paddles across the canoe and just go with the flow. Our freedom allows us to lean to either side and peer down into the clear water. The long strings of moss and other submerged green plants are a delicious sight for eyes accustomed to the dull browns of winter. Occasionally we notice small trout take flight as they rise to a hatch of tiny insects. The jaunt ends too soon and we feel a twinge of disappointment when the springwater vanishes as it mixes with the murky river. We resume paddling and head down the Snake.

Beth and I remain on the side of the river across from another hot springs resort and residences situated between the highway and riverbank. The landscape appears much less civilized over here, and the trees, shrubs, and cattails along the shore keep enticing us with the prospect of wildlife. A few more pairs of geese scold us and we spy several great blue herons, propelled by elegant, unhurried wing beats, that float silently above the river. One of the most notable sights of the day comes when we pass within fifty yards of a bald eagle perched in a tree towering over another spring-fed creek. Again detouring and moving against the channel's flow, we soon realize what lured the iconic bird—the water flows through a fish hatchery. After making a U-turn and starting our drift back down, we notice occasional pieces of farm-raised trout resting on the bottom of the channel.

The final section of our float passes with little fanfare. We stroke across the river at a long diagonal toward our takeout. After having covered a half-dozen miles in the canoe and being confined to it for about the same number of hours, our concern about missing something else has faded. Passing underneath the bridge that carries Highway 30, however, furnishes one last point of interest. As we navigate the steel pylons that rise from the water to support the road, I think about the number of times, well over a hundred over the past half century, that I have crossed this bridge inside a vehicle. Being elevated above the river has given me countless opportunities to glance down and briefly consider the surrounding waterscape. My new perspective gained over our day, and during this moment as we slip through the bridge's shadow, has helped satisfy that curiosity.

This morning we had considered a hike along the river's Upper Salmon Falls, our creek's namesake, once our float trip ended. As we pull the canoe from the water, drive our car back to retrieve the truck, and then return to pick up our vessel, the subject doesn't even come up. After we get everything either tied down or stashed away, I point to a historic steel bridge stretched across the river a half mile downstream. The structure serves as the trek's starting point, but we agree to make the journey another day. The delay seems wise for another reason besides our lack of energy and desire. The trip through that landscape deserves a separate and focused contemplation.

Chapter 5

FEBRUARY 28

Beth and I return a few days later but drive past our canoe trip's takeout and head straight for Owsley Bridge. Completed in 1921 and listed on the National Register of Historic Places, the steel span once served as the only means to cross the Snake River, besides local ferries, for forty miles in either direction. Its fifteen-foot width points back to earlier times and smaller automobiles; two vehicles abreast can now barely be accommodated. Even though the bridge is seldom used, we check for oncoming traffic before proceeding across the rough asphalt. While the road surface gives us little concern, we begin to consider the bridge's condition after noticing widespread splotches of rust on its steel frame. I reply in the affirmative when asked if the structure is safe, but still cannot help but look down and wonder how deep the river might be.

We park in a turnout near the bridge and walk downstream toward Upper Salmon Falls Dam. Discussions began almost a century ago about harnessing the river and utilizing the near hundred-foot drop in elevation over a series of cascades to produce hydroelectric power. It took twenty years and a failed attempt at securing financial backers before the dam was completed in 1937. The diversion forces much of the Snake River into a large concrete canal that parallels the south channel. After going through one powerhouse that contains a turbine spun by the water's descent, electricity is created. The flow is then rerouted into another canal and the process repeated.

The dam leaves the river's north channel exposed and nearly dry during normal years, although signs warn us, "Danger: This area may be flooded at any time." Beth and I leave the trail to investigate and observe dozens of boulders scattered by the Bonneville Flood both above and below the historic high-water mark. The immense release of water occurred only about fifteen thousand years ago near the end of the last ice age. Lake Bonneville, of which Great Salt Lake now remains, had risen and pushed up against a set of hills stacked along the current Idaho-Utah border. When a portion of the land barrier gave way, the result produced an event that cannot be rated as anything less than epic. After finding its way to the Snake River corridor, the rush of water continued westward for two months. The flood added to the height of Shoshone Falls as it tore away bedrock and deepened the canyon downstream. Other landscape removal included the stripping away of topsoil from over fifty square miles along the north side of the river.

The scattering of rocks that Beth and I meander through, once pieces of angular basalt, were rounded and smoothed after being rolled for miles like pebbles. Only a few of the largest boulders, some as tall as me, now remain below the bank where the once "normal" Snake River filled the channel during its highest springtime flows. The terrain has been scoured down to bedrock over the eons, its sharp edges polished and sculpted into countless curves. We step down into the upper level of the watercourse and walk where anadromous fish once swam.

The salmonids came in the form of two species and three distinct runs over the course of a year. Steelhead trout arrived in the frigid waters of April and May. Chinook salmon then came to southern Idaho in two waves: the first appeared during the tail end of the steelhead run, and the second showed up from September through November. Nearing the end of their six-hundred-mile river journey up the Columbia and Snake Rivers, the fish encountered their last pair of major hurdles at Lower and Upper Salmon Falls. With only a few miles between the two sets of cascades, navigating them must have been quite taxing—especially considering that the finned creatures had not eaten since leaving the ocean.

Kelly Murphey, my source on topics related to Native Americans, says that archaeological evidence confirms that these fish provided a major source of protein to humans for close to the last 1,500 years. Some use occurred even longer than that, but the amount is difficult to determine because fish bone does not preserve well and very little of significant age turns up anywhere. The 1989 discovery of the Buhl Woman little more than ten miles upstream, buried for 10,600 years, indicated fish were consumed even that long ago.

During the most recent indigenous occupation of the Hagerman Valley, the majority of Western Shoshone and the Bannock left for part of the year, but the river corridor's importance to their survival was significant. The Shoshone identified the fish according to the season of their appearance. The *tahama agai*, or spring salmon (actually steelhead), were relied upon to help end the period of near-starvation that sometimes began when cached roots, seeds, and fish from the autumn harvest started to run out. The timing of the *taza agai*, or summer salmon, meshed with the departure of those people that headed north to dig camas roots. The arrival of the *yuva agai*, or fall salmon, served as a critical run for those returning from the uplands both north and south, who relied on stockpiled fish to help survive the winter.

Harvest from the Snake River was conducted by a variety of means. The strategic placement of rocks combined with the natural arrangement of boulders, along with constructions made of willow or other woody material, were used to create impoundments or diversions that trapped fish. Other fishermen might rely on gear as simple as a jigging hook or as intricate as a hand net. More iconic weapons such as harpoons or spears were also common. The former were sometimes engineered with detachable points connected with stout string. The latter could be held in the water near a fish's anticipated path and then jabbed through its body as it swam upstream. Fisheries that involved the construction of scaffolding to stand on or the creation of diversions were closely guarded. Etiquette reflected that of modern-day fishermen: those who first occupied the runs were given deference until they had taken all the fish they wanted.

When I initially began to wrap my head around the sorting and naming of fish and people, I developed a somewhat idyllic perspective of aboriginal life. The problem for those actually living off the land, however, was that it was not enough to just show up. The steelhead and salmon harvest by the native people did not always come off like clockwork. The runs could fail to show up in a timely manner or they might not arrive in adequate numbers.

That's why, Kelly reminds me, the Ancient Ones exploited their entire environment and sought a variety of foods during their seasonal rounds. The Hagerman Valley offered a landscape several thousand feet in elevation below the rest of southern Idaho or northern Nevada that the natives also frequented. The milder winter by itself increased their chances of survival. That the low-lying crease through the Snake River Plain also contained a substantial flow of water harboring large fish made the corridor a magnet.

The finned creatures that left the ocean and found their way home were only part of the nutritional equation. Living off the land required flexibility as to where and when the natives traveled and how long they might pause at strategic locations. While the people were more concentrated along the river during certain times of the year, the arid landscape and its lean provisions elsewhere required plenty of space between groups usually no larger than independent families.

Kelly points me to the work of Julian Steward, an ethnologist who gathered information about Native Americans that lived in the Great Basin and surrounding areas. Steward's research and conversations with the grandchildren of those who roamed the region culminated in the 1930s with a book that is still considered a definitive study. With climate and topography determining where plants and animals could be found, his concept of human ecology focused on how people adapted and utilized those resources. And while the author painted a sobering picture of the region's inhabitants and its "meager" culture and resources, Kelly believes that the particular time frame available to Steward was not necessarily representative of the population's overall period of occupation. The arrival of Euro-Americans and other factors certainly had an impact on the indigenous cultures.

And when it came down to surviving at what Steward described in grim terms as a "bare subsistence level," Kelly conducted his own trials in living off the land when he was in his twenties. Mostly self-taught from reading but with some learning from others, he would periodically slip into the Salmon Falls Creek area or head west to the Bruneau country and conduct a private search for nourishment. His take on the landscape after those experiences? "I have done enough desert survival in this region to believe that in an average year it was a fairly productive place for a typical family of foragers. It was no Garden of Eden, but it wasn't a bad place to come up with enough food to eat, except during winter."

That dependence on the land makes me wonder: How would it feel to experience a growing hunger, especially during those coldest days? To have survived those extreme conditions, to have rationed your food, but still run out of supplies? To face the uncertainty, to dream about the return of fish, to embrace your people's narratives of the earth and their mythical characters who look out for your well-being? Was it difficult to decide whether to stay, and for how long, or to go and search elsewhere? Perhaps I am foolish to compare my contemporary mindset of never doing without to a culture that had no option but to endure and adapt to the changing landscape. But I cannot help to consider their approach to survival. What did they think? How did they feel?

It's not hard to get lost in thought about those first residents and their finned prey, but the exposed river channel at Upper Salmon Falls does not let me remain in that headspace for long. The smoothed stone that we step on, over, and around amazes us—not often does one get to see what the bottom of a river looks like. The bedrock is fanciful stuff, composed of a jumbled mix of protrusions and crevices and occasional bowls eroded by the endless spinning circle of gravel and small stones. I try to envision the river's swirls, eddies, and waterfalls that once poured over this landscape, but only partly succeed in linking stone with water. The transformed terrain aptly remains a mystery.

The center of the riverbed tempts us closer with a small amount of water that passes through the dam via a three-foot steel pipe. The flow moves nearly undetected across the disfigured basalt, but then makes a picturesque dive into a narrow chasm. We walk up to the edge and cautiously peer into the thirty-foot depth. Wanting to see the other side of what locals now call the "Fall Hole," Beth and I hike upstream fifty yards, walk across a wooden plank above the flow contained in a narrow trough, and head back down. The striking perspective from that side offers us a series of waterfalls that work their way into the single deep gorge that we viewed moments before. We try scrambling downstream through the maze of rocks, but soon run out of real estate when another fissure cuts us off. After soaking up the view, we backtrack and return to the north shore.

Near our position along the vanquished Snake River, a more notable set of explorers once passed through. Looking for a means in 1811 to expand his fur empire from the Great Lakes to the Pacific, John Jacob Astor sent sixty-five people from St. Louis toward the mouth of the Columbia. After reaching the headwaters of the Snake River, the explorers left their horses behind and began a float trip that they hoped would take them to the ocean. That notion quickly ended when a canoe overturned and one man drowned where the river began to drop into a canyon fifteen miles upstream of Shoshone Falls. Abandoning their watercraft and caching some of their supplies, the expedition was forced to proceed on foot. Wilson Price Hunt split the party into three groups, each in search of a route westward.

Hunt took twelve men along the north side of the river, where they stumbled upon Indians near Upper Salmon Falls. After the natives led them a short distance away from the river, the group encountered lodges covered with thick-stemmed grasses and cattails. The leader's observations became the first Western historical and ethnological account of the area. After observing the "wormwood," or sagebrush, that was used for fuel and piled at the lodges' doors, Hunt made note of something else: "About their dwellings were immense quantities of the heads and skins of salmon, the best part of which had been cured, and hidden in the ground."

Nearly out of food and traveling in mid-November through an area with little other wild game, the explorers fed on fish offered by their hosts. After obtaining enough nourishment from the Shoshone people to regain some strength, the Astorians continued their push to the Pacific.

The next summer Robert Stuart, having made a sea voyage to the mouth of the Columbia, took five companions and retraced Hunt's route. At Lower Salmon Falls he found "about one hundred lodges of Shoshonies busily occupied in Killing & drying Fish." Stuart also noted that "Indians in great numbers with their spears swim in, to near the centre of the Falls, where some placing themselves on Rocks & others to their middle in Water, darts on all sides assail the Salmon."

Since Astor's men were the first white people to visit this portion of southern Idaho, I had assumed that they found the Western Shoshone and Bannock in a somewhat pristine condition. According to Kelly, however, the influence of Europeans had found its way to southern Idaho decades earlier and had not benefited the natives gathered along the river seeking salmon.

In the mid-1700s horses arrived on the Great Plains via the Spanish who brought them to the New World a hundred years earlier. After most native people adopted this hooved technology, the traditional relationships between tribes across North America were disrupted and a domino effect created.

Blackfeet and other groups put enough pressure on the Northern Shoshone, the people famous for Sacajawea and assisting Lewis and Clark, for them to start making westward forays. These mounted warriors could travel from Montana and eastern Idaho to the Hagerman Valley with ease to harvest and transport salmon back to their homeland. The mounted Nez Perce even expanded their range and began filtering down from the northwest. Besides competing with the local residents for the finned protein, big game and other food resources were overharvested. The newcomers could easily dominate the horseless natives who utilized the mid-Snake's fishing falls. Some were even kidnapped and taken back as slaves.

The most ominous visitor to the region, however, arrived in the form of disease: by the late 1700s smallpox had played havoc with Native Americans over the entire region. By some estimates 60 percent of the population who chose to remain horseless and live near the river, according to Kelly, had been decimated by disease before the arrival of Hunt. What remained of the local people represented a shadow of what had developed over thousands of years.

Trappers and explorers like Alexander Ross and John Frémont then passed through the area, helping to establish the Snake River Plain as a strategic corridor that linked the Midwest to the Pacific Ocean. Frémont's romantic reports were especially influential in stoking the dreams of eastern residents wanting something more. Following the Oregon Trail from its origins in Independence, Missouri, emigrants flooded through southern Idaho. After crossing the creek where Beth and I had floated our canoe, the route passed near Upper Salmon Falls on the south side of the river. From there the story of the region's original inhabitants played out in much the same manner as it did across the Americas and elsewhere over the world. The arrival of a dominant culture increased the demand for a limited supply of resources and eventually destroyed the dynamic balance the First People had established with their environment.

Conflicts arose along the Snake River and natives were sometimes killed indiscriminately in the name of safety—or sometimes just for sport. Tensions escalated when Indians, now in direct competition for what the land could offer, began stealing from immigrants. Skirmishes broke out and people on both sides died. Relations deteriorated even further, resulting in a pair of massacres by the Indians in the early 1860s.

The military presence at Rock Creek south of Twin Falls was then moved and Fort Reed reestablished near Miracle Hot Springs a few years later. Shortly after their arrival, a troop was sent south in search of Indians. Their three-hundred-mile round-trip into the uplands of both Salmon Falls Creek and Rock Creek to the east allegedly resulted in the killing of three natives, the capture of three more, the destruction of six fisheries, and the driving of the "tribe" into the mountains.

Manifest Destiny had little room for any of the Indian tribes. By the early 1880s the armed conflicts in the West were nearly over and the natives subdued. A few lingered on through the turn of the century, but when the Swan Falls Dam ended the fish runs, their residency effectively ended.

Do we current residents all feel some degree of sympathy for the earth's humans who were forced off their landscape? Probably not. What we do with our complicated past is up to the individual. Whenever I spend time at these falls that were either dewatered or flooded permanently, however, it's impossible for me not to consider the Ancient Ones. I hold no right to claim kinship to those first inhabitants, given my descent from a culture that pushed them away. I do feel, however, something of a connection to them.

For as long as I can remember, my parents collected antique bottles. While the effort was a serious but enjoyable hobby, Mom and Dad each possessed a strong desire to bond with the past. They researched and purchased the glass items through the mail or shows they attended. A couple of decades after my father died, Mom eventually decided to sell most of their bottle collection. Before doing so she asked me if I wanted anything. I chose an amber flask that had been made prior to the Civil War. It still moves me to hold on to something that fragile, to grasp the past and run my fingers over the glass covered with raised embossing that depicts two scenes. One side of the bottle sports an angler standing with a pole in his left hand and a fish in the right. On the other side a man shoots at airborne birds that a pair of dogs have flushed. The two figures do not appear to represent people focused on subsistence; their stovepipe hats and formal jackets make them appear more as gentleman sportsmen.

My justification to sometimes take life from the land is likely much closer to those featured on my hunter-fisherman flask than the Ancient Ones. I have never needed to kill anything in order to survive. I believe in a shared instinct, however, that compels me to try to fit into a wild landscape well enough to successfully take part in the complicated relationship between predator and prey.

I first explored Upper Salmon Falls a decade before Beth and I came here together. In search of something that might provide evidence of the Native Americans' occupation, I brought with me a naïve and romantic perspective. Here on this outcrop or that boulder could have been someone with a spear searching the cascading waters, ready to fling a weapon. He is in the same instant both hunter and fisherman. I still hang on to that iconic scene, but it's since evolved a bit. The background is now blurred with the arrival of white men.

Beth and I meander farther downriver as our course takes us to more spots where the lives of humans and fish once intersected. We discover waterfalls that, unlike their upstream counterparts, generously spread their liquid across broad rock shelves. The stone creations along the riverbed continue to amaze us; no two appear the same, but all display the wear of water and time. After several hundred yards the drainage levels out and we are left with a single chasm a couple hundred feet wide and deeper than anything else yet seen.

More of Upper Salmon Falls remains to be seen, but not on this day. We have run out of the capacity to absorb much more, but achieved our goal in bearing witness to the riverscape that our creek was named after. Like the horseless nomads of long ago, we now are ready to walk south into the high desert. Before we leave and start planning that journey, there remains one last task to complete here. I make my customary pilgrimage to a place where my fingers can touch the past written by humans not on glass, but stone. Instead of the usual silent homage, I am this time able to share with Beth, "Yes, they were here."

Chapter 6

MARCH 5

Miracle Hot Springs, the put-in for our float trip, again serves as a starting point. This time we walk down the highway and pause on the bridge that we floated under three weeks earlier. Looking down at the boulders and trees that gave us our first challenge before the canoe hardly got wet, I wonder about that spot. Would this bird's-eye view prior to our departure been helpful or were we better off not knowing what we were getting into? There is little time to ponder the question, however, as we first hear and then turn to see a car speeding down the highway in our direction. We scamper off the bridge and head upstream.

While there is always something gained with any undertaking that pulls me out my comfort zone, like our canoe adventure, the return to purposeful walking brings me pleasure. And even though the Snake River and Hagerman Valley's rich history and geology captured my imagination last month, part of me is ready to retreat into a desert landscape with fewer human complications.

That desire is not granted right away. After departing from a paved road that leads up to the Magic Water farming project, we are forced to navigate around a patchwork of private property intermingled with public ground controlled by the Bureau of Land Management (BLM).

Matching up lines on our map with actual barbed wire fences that likely serve as boundaries between the two becomes a little confusing, but we do make certain to give a wide berth to several houses and one barking dog. Our setting feels a little calmer once we move past human creations and glimpse a familiar, yet natural, construction in the form of rimrock along the skyline.

Happy to escape civilization, we enter the mouth of the canyon. The area isn't devoid of evidence from mankind—we find a scattering of empty shotgun shells ejected from firearms swung on waterfowl—but our steps are taking us in the right direction. While hunting season ended several months ago, the evidence of winter's chill hangs on in the form of ice clinging to the canyon's lower, shaded walls.

The unfolding leaf buds of golden currants serve as a counteroffer in recognition of the near arrival of spring. One of the first shrubs in the region to show life, the plants look to be at least a week ahead of those at home, which is twenty miles away and five hundred feet higher in elevation. Other vegetation that has lain dormant is also beginning to green up, especially in those niches that favor a southern exposure. We stop and peer down into the cured stalks of last year's bunchgrasses and confirm the presence of tender shoots pushing upward. On the bare ground between those plants, we notice an occasional native bee warming in the sun as it readies for flight. Another indicator of a change in season comes in the form of a meadowlark's cheerful serenade. We both remark how long it's been since our ears were exposed to their distinctive melody.

When the canyon upstream begins to take shape and looks like it might envelop us enough to make an exit challenging, we begin an angled ascent. After huffing and puffing our way out—another seasonal indicator seems to be that neither of us are in great shape—a clear view back into the Hagerman Valley serves as our reward. We take a moment to reflect on last month's adventures before making an about-face to walk along the edge of the canyon.

I hang on to one detail from that past—we now follow the footsteps of Native Americans as they too slipped away from the confines of the river valley and headed south. The anthropologist Julian Steward noted that the Shoshone and other Indians traveled along the edge of the Salmon Falls Creek gorge between the valley's winter camps and the southern uplands along the Idaho-Nevada border. Families broke away from the large social groups and began seeking berries, roots, and game which would become more plentiful as the altitude and rainfall increased. Our trek is likely a little earlier in the year than when traveled by the natives, and the aim of our search is certainly tied more to our mental and emotional well-being rather than survival. Still, I would like to think that an immersion into the desert plain and escaping concentrations of people might provide something in common. I also feel satisfaction that my favorite choice of transport, swinging one leg in front of the other, aligns with that of the pedestrian Shoshone.

One more character comes to mind from the past in the form of a man who wrote perhaps the most famous essay about foot travel. Henry David Thoreau asserted in "Walking" that the movement should not be dismissed as an ordinary activity, but rather be honored as soul-enriching. He believed that his favorite term for the art form, *sauntering*, had its roots in the Middle Ages and referred to people searching for the Holy Land. He encouraged readers to make every walk a crusade. Ideally a walker should never retrace their steps or circle back to a starting point, but go forth "in the spirit of undying adventure, never to return."

Sauntering should be initiated, he emphasized, in the opposite direction of the comforts of home or town and its practical matters. But it took more than just putting distance between one's physical body and civilization. A commitment to staying present and relying on the powers of observation were required. While Thoreau spent a lifetime striving for a connection to his environment, he wrote about once being alarmed after having walked a mile without getting there in spirit. "What business have I in the woods, if I am thinking of something out of the woods?"

And so Beth and I saunter away in our own fashion on a one-way journey that should cover about eight miles. While absent of trees, our setting of sagebrush—called "wormwood" by explorer Wilson Price Hunt—on our right side and a vertical drop-off on the left suits us just fine. And while he never had the chance to walk through the West, I think Thoreau might approve.

As we enter into a rhythm, delight fills me with the prospect of sharing a long hike with my wife. After meeting thirty-five years ago at the University of Idaho, our first meaningful conversations focused on backpacking. We traded narratives of experiences arrived at by far different means. My father took my two brothers and me on our first overnighter as preteens. Instead of hiking upward, we dropped down to a lake nestled below a fire lookout perched on top of Trinity Mountain southeast of Boise. From there our family made at least one trek per year into the several mountain ranges that rise on either side of the headwaters of the Salmon River in central Idaho. The escape from the farm and August heat into a wild, elevated haven became each summer's highlight.

Beth was raised in Cleveland, Ohio, with not a mountain in sight, but a cross-country move as a teenager placed her in Boise. During her senior year in high school, she took a backpacking class and made her first overnight trip into an iconic mountain range already familiar to me. The next year as a college freshman, she again ventured into alpine country above Hells Canyon in eastern Oregon. I was stunned and ecstatic to meet a backpacking girl—the odds of that combination seemed rather low. Our parallel adventures contributed to the initial bond that ultimately bestowed me with a lifelong partner. Together we explored a handful of mountain ranges new to both of us, as well as the Sawtooths, the one that we had encountered separately. Beth and I even slipped into the White Clouds on a three-day trip while she was seven months pregnant.

As the decades passed, carrying gear and sleeping on hard ground became increasingly uncomfortable; the frequency of overnight trips together now had waned to almost nothing. Day hikes are still common, but even that kind of joint jaunt had not occurred since the previous summer. I cannot think of anything I would rather be doing than spending a pleasant late-winter day with Beth along this canyon. Also, as she is only a few months retired, I trust our outing might carry additional significance for her.

A couple of miles upstream from Miracle Hot Springs, the canyon narrows and deepens into a stunning vision. I cannot help but repeatedly focus on the opposite rim, drop my gaze to the wildness below, and then look back up to the farms crowding the canyon's edge. A few of the crop fields are populated by center-pivot irrigation systems; mentally processing the presence of iron and mankind's imprint so close to the natural world keeps my focus shifting. In several spots the creek benefits from seepage entering through the canyon's porous rock walls. The source of the water is likely not from the noticeable sprinklers, but rather flood irrigation on some fields that saturates the soil and travels downward through the bedrock before moving sideways into the canyon. In turn some of that groundwater that flows into the creek gets pumped out of the canyon, this time to the opposite side, and is used for irrigation one last time.

Our forward progress along the twisting rim is occasionally compromised by small ravines that enter from the Magic Water tract. These dips in the landscape force us into a looping contour through them to minimize the tiring effect of too many abrupt up-and-downs. Our short detours bring us back for one more new perspective of the canyon and the rural landscape spread along its opposite side. With each reunion I feel a little envious looking at those farms. How satisfying would that feel to have land bordering this gorge? Potential access into its chambers would be a bonus, but just owning a spot that provides that kind of view would be superb. I wonder briefly if the perspective would become such a common occurrence that the canyon's appeal might be lost, but quickly dismiss the notion.

Our hike continues into the afternoon and delivers us to another of the drainage's unique geological features. Over the course of a mile, the canyon's east face has periodically broken away and settled downward, leaving a jumbled landform of broken basalt and soil, most of which grows sagebrush, spread below the rim. The displacement of material separates the retreating rimrock from the creek by nearly a half mile—making the canyon wider here than anywhere else on the entire stretch from Salmon Dam to where it ends near the river.

The landslides have likely occurred as long as the canyon has been around, but two major events took place during the last eighty years.

Over the course of three weeks during the summer of 1937, just over ten acres of farmland along the rim slumped down into the canyon. The landslide not only seized the attention of local residents, but with stories appearing in newspapers across the country, drew visitors from every state in the nation. The *Twin Falls Times* reported that during the first year almost twelve thousand people paid the landowner a fee of twenty-five cents for the privilege of seeing the phenomenon. While H. A. Robertson was initially hesitant to allow people on his land for safety reasons, the new edge of the canyon was soon fenced off, guards and guides hired to control foot traffic, and an observation tower constructed to enhance the view. Outside attempts to capitalize on the event were also undertaken. Thousands of postcards were distributed by a pair of amateur photographers, and at least one pilot flew his airplane over the canyon, two passengers per flight, after taking off from Twin Falls.

Henceforth known as Sinking Canyon, the area remained relatively stable until another shift in the earth took place not long ago. In 1999 rock climbers testing their ability on the basalt cliffs a half mile upstream from the first event began noticing something strange—their finger holds in the rock had widened to openings they could stick their fists into.

Around the same time, Joe and Cheryl Gellings's hired man reported that a crack in the ground had appeared in a dry pasture adjacent to the canyon. It was hard for the couple to not miss the irony. When they first saw the ranch's layout a few years earlier, they immediately fell in love with the place and knew they wanted to move their purebred Salers herd of cattle there from eastern Idaho. The name of their seed stock operation was even changed to reflect the landscape. "We thought it was a no-brainer to call our business 'Sunken Canyon' because it was done sinking at the time," said Joe.

After the move, the Gellingses were confronted with the aftermath of the 1937 event, which was also within the ranch's confines, when a couple of cows perished after falling into fissures that the previous owner had apparently not completely filled. But still, they thought, that was all in the past.

But what about this new crack opening up on land south of their house? It just kept spreading and eventually separated acreage similar to the previous event. The isolated block of land began to subside and, along with the canyon terrain below it, slip in the direction of the creek. "It moved slowly but on some days you could tell how much. We could hear rocks falling down into the crack and see puffs of dust rising out of it," Joe said. Over time the couple witnessed the land's western movement first impede and then back up Salmon Falls Creek for a considerable distance.

Once word got out about the event and a newspaper story described the possibility of a flood if the new dam on the creek broke, the mood changed. "Everybody got stirred up and all sorts of people wanted to see it," Joe said. The public sought access through the ranch for the chance to see the landslide up close. The demand was intense but the landowners resisted. "We just couldn't allow it—the liability was too great. Dealing with that part of it was just awful."

In 2001, during the peak of the event, federal agencies began monitoring the movement and the next year turned that responsibility over to Idaho State University. A thesis by graduate student Steven Dorsch offers an explanation of the event. This most recent landslide, which likely began several years before it was first detected, developed in the same manner as its Depression-era neighbor. Ordinary basalt flows comprise the canyon's upper strata, but on this stretch they sit on top of poorly structured sedimentary deposits. The instability there leads to a major fracture that works its way to the surface of the ground. When the block of land becomes isolated and cannot be supported by its unstable foundation, it slowly breaks away and slides into the canyon. With the head wall pushing both laterally and downward, the toe of the landslide rotates upward. In the last event the west edge of the mass ended at the creek and lifted its channel about thirteen feet. By the time the level of the creek had risen high enough to cut a new course, a mile-long reservoir had been formed.

During this latest transformation, but before the Bureau of Land

Management closed the area for safety reasons due to its unsteady state, a little exploring seemed in order. I first spent time examining the deep split from a safe distance on public land before proceeding down to investigate the crumpled landscape. A multitude of small cracks running across the ground and periodic bulges hinted of topography under tension. After scrambling over the disarrangement, both present and past, I reached the spot where the bottom of the canyon had risen and dammed the creek. While fascinated enough by the whole scene to be motivated to walk the length of the impoundment, the urge to retreat won out. Although I tried to reassure myself over several hours that I remained perfectly safe amidst the evolving terrain, I had not fully bought into that notion. The relief felt after climbing out of the canyon and returning to flat, dependable-looking ground remains a strong memory.

As Beth and I walk the opposite rim almost fifteen years later, no such anxiety exists—as well as any desire to observe Sinking Canyon from anywhere but above. With mid-afternoon upon us we do not, in fact, feel much of anything besides being tired and footsore. Our focus increasingly leaves the altered landscape as we search inland for our pickup that we dropped off earlier. Once it comes into view we angle to the west and plod along for another half hour. Our projected eight-mile hike ends up being about ten, but Beth has impressed me. I don't believe that she has ever hiked this far in one day and did so with little preparation.

Chapter 7

MARCH 8

Three days later Beth and I leave our car at the parking lot below Balanced Rock and drive back to our previous endpoint. Our route again crowds the rim so that we can see as much of the upper end of Sinking Canyon as possible. We bear witness to the creek-turned-lake, taking stock of the skeletons of sagebrush and other drought-tolerant shrubs and trees whose roots could not endure the rising water level. Some of the victims remain standing in isolation, knee-deep in water twenty feet from the edge of the new lake. The balance between plant, soil, and water, once considered stable, has been disrupted.

Changes in the natural world enable some organisms to prosper as others perish. Through binoculars I can see new willows growing along the lake where before they would not have found enough water. Other hydrophytic vegetation likely inhabits the moist ribbon of silt loam along the bank, but the scene is too far away to differentiate among species. While taking one last look at the lake and pondering the steps to its creation, I know enough to appreciate this wreck of a landscape. It's a rare thing when we humans have the chance to bear witness to a geologic event that occurs in a noticeable manner. Had I lived in the Magic Valley back in 1937, I can see myself paying twenty-five cents and climbing that observation tower to get a good look at the "first" Sinking Canyon.

A mile upstream we pass another spot where the opposite rim seems to have slid down into the bottom of the canyon, but not nearly on the same scale. The creek looks like it again had been shoved away from its former route. Even from our lofty perch, some of the channel lies hidden as its fluid bounces through the crumpled canyon floor.

We step into a new environment when the canyon makes a ninety-degree bend to the west. The now south-facing rimrock, bathed in the late-morning sun, prompts us to remove a layer of clothing. After we disturb several lizards that are also taking advantage of the warmth, Beth begins to stalk them in hopes of a photo opportunity. After a few of the reptiles cooperate with a brief pose, we consider resuming our pace but find our momentum has gone missing. We instead opt for a brief halt and choose to eat lunch while sitting on an overhang along the rim.

The perch provides us with a front-row seat from where we observe a pair of red-tailed hawks. Their call—often substituted in movies or television shows for the bald eagle's less resonant chirp—gives away their presence as they float in lazy spirals above us. Without warning one of the mating pair occasionally dives down several hundred feet into the canyon's void.

The springlike heat seems to energize other wildlife. After our hike resumes we flush several cottontails and watch them zigzag through the sagebrush before finding safety in the cracks of the broken rimrock. Around the next bend we jump a dozen deer from a small draw that empties into the canyon. They appear frantic during the first few moments of their escape, bounding away almost like the rabbits, but quickly settle down and stop to watch us. On separate occasions we then get glimpses of the region's two largest winged carnivores: a turkey vulture and a golden eagle. While the vulture likely just arrived from a warmer climate, I wonder if the eagle might be the same bird seen twice in January. It's likely not a coincidence since Balanced Rock, as an eagle flies, is now only a couple of miles away.

Our constant companion during the day, not in terms of a single creature but as a species, is the meadowlark. It seems like we are never beyond earshot of the serenading bird and at times approach close enough to enjoy what feels like a private performance. While not their intended audience, we hang on to the illusion that the melodies are for our ears only. And after walking into the middle of the afternoon, any perceived encouragement is welcome. As was the case three days ago, I seemed to have again underestimated our hiking distance.

We remain loyal to the canyon for as long as possible, but when within a half mile of the point on the rim that overlooks the road crossing, we instead angle westward and head directly toward Balanced Rock. As we cut through the sculpted outcrops, which I last saw covered with snow six weeks earlier, we make a small detour so as not to disturb a family of four hikers enjoying the landscape.

Beth and I then crawl underneath the big rock and slide down the final steep slope to the parking lot. The novel approach and arrival feel odd, but only until the car's engine turns over. We so welcome the idea of getting off our feet and letting something with a motor do the work. On the drive back to our starting point at Sinking Canyon, Beth barely has time to remove her shoes and socks and cool off her newest blisters. It takes less than fifteen minutes to return to our point of departure from seven hours earlier.

Chapter 8

MARCH 16–17

The dream once shared with my father of spending a day to hike through the canyon from Lilly Grade to Balanced Rock never quite left me. Perhaps deep down I knew how unrealistic our trip would have been, but admitting to that might have meant letting a piece of him slip away. Even when my January hike along the rim between the two crossings forced me to admit that a day trip was not possible, I still held on to hiking the stretch in one attempt. It only seemed fitting then that with the next part of my project focused on that same piece of canyon, I might honor our vision by backpacking through the canyon's confines with my wife.

In trying to fit the trek around both work and family commitments, we schedule it for two days in mid-March. As the target date gets closer, the weather forecast calls for one unseasonably warm afternoon followed by a cold front and high winds on St. Patrick's Day. We consider postponing, but then decide to seize the window of opportunity. I reason that any day spent recreating in the outdoors, no matter what the weather outlook, has to be better than passing that time stuck in the office or at home. And with the protection that being in the bottom of a four-hundred-foot deep gorge would offer, surely we can handle a little wind. Right?

Besides the predicted change in weather, another issue arises. During several conversations with local residents, my idea of a journey inside the canyon is met with skepticism. While the sampling size is small, the consensus seems to be that a hike is not possible without encountering several creek-side cliffs that likely will not grant access around them. I assume that one such barrier is the outcrop that turned me back six weeks ago, but no one can provide details about where the trouble spots lurk. And despite assuming a second obstacle might lie upstream from my point of defeat, I remain optimistic that a passage through the canyon exists.

After saying good-bye to our son Keegan, the echoes from the slam of the car trunk and the hum of the vehicle driving back through the county park become our last link to humanity. A half mile later Beth and I have little trouble traversing, even with backpacks, the first ledge that angles into the creek. I then revisit the juniper snag while filling her in on the puzzle of its journey and resting place between boulders. Twenty minutes later we arrive at the rock outcrop that ended my upstream trek. Nothing has changed, of course, since I last lingered there; the trail still dead-ends where the rock face plummets down to meet the water's edge. Our only two options are to get wet or go up.

This time, however, I'm accompanied by a real climber—someone who has ascended several peaks in the Sawtooths and frequented southern Idaho's famous City of Rocks. With her pack still strapped to her back, Beth easily scampers up the rock face and then offers assurance from a ledge fifteen feet above me. Before starting I drop my bulky backpack to the ground, tie one end of a thin rope to it, and toss the other end to my wife. Buoyed by her presence and advice, I shimmy up a three-sided chimney—the same one I attempted in January and navigated as a teenager—and soon join her. The most difficult task then amounts to pulling my thirty-pound pack up without snagging it on several protrusions jutting from the side of the cliff.

After extricating ourselves from the top of the outcrop, we contour around the canyon's steep side slope and work our way back down to the creek. I am encouraged by our success, especially when remembering how pitiful I felt six weeks earlier after my forced retreat. Now past a major hurdle that severely limits access upstream, we savor the realization that not many have traveled this faint path. Even though a tamer world looms above us just beyond the rim, it feels like we could be hiking through a remote wilderness.

My state of satisfaction soon vanishes, however, when Beth's feet roll out from underneath her while crossing a steep patch of scree. While she gets up quickly and is unhurt, I am reminded about not getting too comfortable with our freedom and isolation. Relishing those qualities also comes with the reality that help will not be immediately available in case something unforeseen happens. It's not possible to just call for assistance since the depth of this wild setting also ensures a lack of cell phone coverage.

But the acceptance of risk also brings with it a sense of liberation and the reward of being able to experience a new landscape. In the winter when I bore witness to this stretch of creek from above, the canyon had been easy to appreciate as part of a grand panorama. Hiking through the bottom of the gorge, now only able to see as far as the next bend, offers a more intimate experience. And having the opportunity to share it with my wife makes the outing that much better.

The variety of wildlife inside the canyon comes as a surprise. I could depend on the presence of ducks, mostly mallards and a few teal and nearly all in breeding pairs, which periodically lift off the water and escape upstream. But many of the other encounters are not expected. On two occasions goose couples perched high atop the rock pillars eyeball us as we pass underneath them, but only after having also given us a scolding that echoes off the canyon's walls. We catch a glimpse of a muskrat making a hurried underwater cruise and in several places find thin willow stumps left by beavers. Quail and gray partridge occasionally flush from the currant and sumac shrub thickets bordering the creek, and several chukars take flight from halfway up the canyon's slope. On one occasion we first hear and then spy a pair of yipping coyotes below the opposite rim. Above all of us red-tailed hawks soar in elegant spirals.

While the animals inhabiting the canyon environment move about with ease, we two humans trying to fit temporarily into the landscape do so with much effort and little grace. Progress is gained in slow increments that follow the crooked line of the creek. Several times the canyon's sweeping slope runs nearly to the edge of the stream, leaving us to hike on ankle-bending side hills often covered with bouldered talus. Where a generous width of soil does exist along the stream channel, the corridor sometimes supports shrubs dense enough to make pushing through them a chore.

The rich mix of rock, wildlife, and vegetation offering the promise of spring accompanies us for several miles. Just as I begin to take the landscape for granted, however, we walk into another world.

Enclosed in our engaging bubble, I had not thought once about my January hike and walking several miles through an environment compromised by the wildfire from two summers ago. I had forgotten about the burn working its way into the canyon and how devastated the landscape looked from the rim. And so I am again stunned by the transformation. Charred branches of sumac litter the canyon floor, and only stumps of sagebrush remain. The number of junipers killed by the fire, however, shocks me. While some survived, most are reduced to skeletons, both standing and prone. In places cheatgrass and other resourceful annual weeds have begun to stake claim.

But the news is not entirely bad. The fire seems to have had little long-term effect on the willow thickets and cattails and other moisture-loving plants residing next to the creek. The heat and flames likely consumed them also that summer, but by the following spring their energy stored underground again pushed life upward. And upon closer inspection farther away from the stream, we find sumacs that have sprouted from blackened stubs and tiny leaves of golden currants pushing up through the ash. The battle for vegetative dominance continues.

After spending most of the day following the canyon's meanders at an average speed of about a mile per hour, we reach the mouth of Devil Creek. Since we are near the midpoint of our trip and this area captured my attention like no other during my first trek along the rim, it seems like a practical spot to make camp. Surrounded by blackened sagebrush, we pitch the tent in a small open spot near the creek.

While Beth crawls inside to relax, the feel of not having a backpack hanging from my shoulders motivates me to explore. The dry Devil Creek channel lures me upstream to where I meet a line of live junipers not touched by the fire. Easy forward progress soon ends when the creek bed becomes filled with large boulders that require me to climb over them. I again remember how enticing this area had looked from above during my winter trek. Now that I am here in the middle of it and at the end of a long day, it has taken on a different feel. With my interest now satisfied, I circle back to camp.

While little time exists to do much more—official sundown is an hour away even though the orb had long ago disappeared behind the canyon rim—I utilize the waning light to fish. I soon find out that stuffing the spinning reel and small telescoping rod deep into my pack was worth the effort. While the thickets of last year's dried cattails make accessing the creek difficult and my feet are soon soaked, I am rewarded with two full-bodied, beautiful trout. With no need to kill and eat, I slip them back into the creek.

Beth and I lounge in our tent and enjoy the last of the twilight and warmth left over from the day. We crawl into our sleeping bags before nine o'clock and speculate on what the next day might bring. The last weather forecast available to us called for the cold front to arrive well before daybreak. The prediction then had become more disconcerting: high temperatures might not reach forty degrees, and wind gusts would likely push fifty miles per hour.

During the day as we enjoyed the warm sun and remained engaged in such a captivating landscape, it had been easy to not think about the upcoming change. As I lay awake questioning our plans, however, my thoughts turn toward potential escape routes if conditions became unbearable. The canyon does not offer many departure points up through the east rim, but a few do exist that would allow us out. From there we could walk a mile to the nearest public road or even to Kelly Murphey's house. While part of me cannot imagine a worst-case scenario that would force us to abort our journey, my anxiety-prone mind cannot help but go there. Lying on the hard ground and unable to sleep during the literal calm before the storm, I wait.

At three-thirty in the morning our tent begins to flutter as the cold front announces its arrival. By five o'clock the roar of the wind seems to mock our presence, and within an hour a brief rain squall pelts the outer fabric. A peek from the tent at daybreak reveals a drastic change in the world. I search for the memory of yesterday's fine weather, but it seems to have been swept away.

I have visions of the tent pulling its stakes and spinning through the air like Dorothy's house in *The Wizard of Oz* if we venture out, so we stay inside and do as much packing as possible. We then empty our shelter and wrestle it to the ground before a gust gets the chance to toss it toward the creek. Once we finish cramming everything back where it came from, except for several layers of clothing not needed before, we begin the second day's journey. While not exactly happy to be hiking again, we are relieved to no longer feel like hostages inside the tent.

I had hoped that after returning to the canyon's normal width, which had broadened where it accepts Devil Creek, we might find better protection from the gale. In most spots that proves true, but in other places the wind seems to accelerate as if being concentrated through a wind tunnel. The only positive spin I can grasp is that the force pushes at us from behind. Walking into its teeth would make our outing feel like cruel and unusual punishment.

Within an hour of our start we encounter steep, rocky terrain next to the creek that hints at blocking forward progress. We begin to angle uphill in hopes of going above and around the cliffs, but the farther we go the bleaker our new option appears. Our position also exposes us to that much more wind. After progressing about halfway up the side of the canyon, Beth shouts over the gale the very words that I am thinking: "Where are we going?"

I knew that within a few miles of leaving camp we had to cross Salmon Falls Creek and then eventually connect with a faint trail on the east side. It's now obvious that should have already happened. As we reverse course I can't help but laugh at myself—turning back into the wind means temporarily saying good-bye to the morning's lone silver lining that I could find. The gusts seem to enjoy testing our balance a second time as we again navigate the same angled rock piles. After fifteen minutes of backtracking, we find a crossing concealed in the cattails and tall grasses. We hop over the cluster of boulders that had long ago rolled into the water and again press upstream.

As the trek unfolds, the weather fails to improve. The wind continues to howl and my thermometer reports the temperature has indeed dropped down into the high thirties. We have no need, even with our exertions, to remove gloves, stocking caps, and the extra layers of clothing. Snowflakes begin to mix with the tumbleweeds that parachute off the rim hundreds of feet above us. When we look up to see what else might be blowing in the wind, we notice clouds of dust and ash being pushed over the rim after their removal from the bare desert plain. Under different circumstances the dramatic air show might have prompted an element of wonder. The visual instead just adds to the feeling that the earth has somehow slipped off its axis.

Except for a few ducks, the wildlife that shared the canyon with us the previous day has vanished. Only we, it feels like, don't have enough sense to hunker down and wait out the storm. We try taking some satisfaction at seeing several unique rock formations, deep pools in the creek, and other intriguing landforms. As we pass by them I make a mental note to return and explore this stretch on a day defined more by pleasure than survival.

Around noon Beth and I take refuge behind a boulder resting on the creek's narrow floodplain. Our lunch is consumed quickly, not out of hunger, but in an attempt to keep dirt off the food and out of our mouths. We discuss the possibility of leaving the canyon at some point and walking along the rim for the last mile to Lilly Grade. I do not mention my hope to navigate the entire length inside the canyon to fulfill what now feels like an ill-advised obligation to honor a ghost. Nor do I bring up my desire to reach a spot where I remember seeing my father's grin after he caught a trout on our final outing together. Sentiment does not carry much weight while stuck deep in the canyon and trying to endure such a raw day. We agree that whatever route gets us home the quickest will be the one to pursue.

Soon after our break we reach the stretch of canyon most familiar to me from my teenaged outings that began at Lilly Grade. Much of this section escaped the last fire and so is still crowded with vegetation. While part of me is happy to see landscape in more of an unblemished state, our pace slows considerably. Much of the trail is obscured by a tangle of robust sage and four-wing saltbrush hiding an assortment of small boulders that on occasion collide with our knees and shins.

After spending almost two hours wading through a mile of mostly brush and rock, Beth and I agree to having had enough of our canyon experience. With a break in the rim up ahead, we begin a steeply angled ascent that makes us stop often to catch our breath. During our climb we receive a glimpse of the Lilly Grade road that verifies less than two miles of walking remains. Right before we slip through an opening in the rock wall that allows entrance onto the desert plain, we take one last view down. As spectacular as the canyon still appears, I have never felt more relieved to escape its reach. And while my attachment to this particular stretch will eventually entice me back down, I cannot imagine returning anytime soon.

I phone my mother to let her know about our status and discuss a pickup time and place. In conveying her and Keegan's concern for us, she confirms that winds gusts up to sixty-five miles per hour were being reported across southern Idaho. The gale had been forceful enough to tip over a couple of semitrailer trucks on two different bridges that cross the Snake River Canyon near Twin Falls. The trucks had fortunately remained on the spans, which were quickly shut down for the afternoon.

As fiercely as the wind had pushed at us in the canyon, we confirm that it did offer more protection than up here on top. As we walk toward our destination, an occasional gust shoves us from behind with enough push to propel our top-heavy profiles into a trot that lasts several steps. The extra momentum does help us cover the flat ground faster than I had estimated, and we reach the top of Lilly Grade ten minutes before Mom is supposed to arrive. After shedding our packs we lean them up against a barbed wire fence to create some shelter before we plop down on the ground to wait.

A pickup soon drives by and its two occupants wave at us before continuing down into the canyon, but after a couple of minutes they return and pull over. The driver rolls his window down and shouts over the wind, "Are you two okay?" He probably would like to add a couple more questions like "Are you crazy?" and "What are you doing out here on such a crappy day?" but to his credit he does not. Once we assure him that we are fine, we admit to hiking in the canyon and that someone is coming to take us home. After we thank them for stopping, they turn the truck back around and head down Lilly Grade. At least our brief exchange had given them something to talk about as they make their own voyage, albeit much briefer and more comfortable, through the canyon.

Chapter 9

APRIL 13

The notion of hiking the length of the Salmon Falls Creek watershed came with a few conditions. Once my wanderings near Balanced Rock, the canoe trip, and our inspection of the falls on the Snake River were done, I intended to head upstream and walk next to or sometimes inside the creek's canyon. To reach the headwaters in Nevada's Jarbidge Mountains before snow started falling, it would take about one trek per month. The logistics for tackling each stretch seemed simple: begin the next hike where the previous one left off.

The preparations for the next outing upstream from Lilly Grade are a little more complicated than before, but come together without a hitch. On Friday evening I stash our overnight gear halfway along our weekend route. Beth and I can then enjoy a tent and sleeping bags along with extra clothes, food, and water but without having to carry them on our backs for twenty miles. After leaving the supplies in a remote patch of sagebrush, I meet Keegan back at the main gravel road. From there we drive in tandem to within a few miles of Salmon Dam, where we leave the pickup.

The next morning greets us with temperatures in the upper thirties and a stiff wind that I don't recall being part of the previous day's forecast. While not in the league of the St. Patrick Day's gale, the prospect of spending portions of consecutive overnight hikes putting up with a cold wind does not sound appealing. I suggest to Beth that since we already have a vehicle positioned out near the canyon, perhaps we should consider an alternative. What if Keegan instead drives us to Salmon Dam? We can make a short four-mile hike from there, which is next on our list anyway, and then attempt our two-day trek the following weekend. She readily agrees.

Rather than taking the shorter but mostly graveled road from home to our destination, we opt for Highway 93 that leads toward Nevada. Fifteen miles before Jackpot, we head west from Rogerson and follow a paved road over the top of Salmon Dam. Built over a century ago, the concrete monolith included a roadway on its crest—a first for any North American dam. Completed with a design called a gravity arch, its curve upstream allows the force of the pooled water to be applied through the structure and against the opposing canyon walls. The construction's shape also creates a down pressure that enhances its stability.

While most who cross the dam will think nothing about those forces that keep the concrete compressed into the earth's basalt flows, they will notice the roadway's tight clockwise curve while heading west. To make things more interesting, drivers must also give the right-of-way to oncoming traffic already on the dam since the route is only wide enough for one vehicle. And sometimes the competition to use the single lane is not limited to people.

Since the passage serves as the only place to herd cattle across the drainage for a span of thirty miles, complications can arise when they are trailed over the dam. On the one occasion when I dropped down into the canyon and hiked to the foot of the massive concrete plug, the discovery of a cow carcass puzzled me. I later learned that a driver tried to cross the structure before an entire herd had completed their journey. One unlucky animal panicked and jumped or was crowded over the three-foot-high abutment by her companions.

Our early-morning crossing presents us with neither a vehicle nor bovine in sight. After saying good-bye to our son, Beth and I yank our stocking caps down to minimize our skin's exposure to the headwind and begin hiking downstream. Our bearing feels odd since, other than my New Year's Day jaunt, I have rarely walked in a northerly direction. Another striking difference to the experience is that the canyon does not resemble anything like the V-shaped chasm that has become so familiar to us. The forces of nature in this new environment have carved out a smaller gorge, marked by vertical walls, which fits inside the main canyon's more typical upper slopes.

After scrambling down one those slanted hillsides, we encounter a flat bench that drops vertically to the creek. Our overlook also places us at nearly the same elevation as the dam's crest and offers a clear view of the entire construction that rises little more than a quarter mile away. From our perspective it's easy to see why that especially narrow gap in the canyon was filled with concrete.

But that decisively human action did not mark the first time that a thickening liquid blocked the flow of Salmon Falls Creek. According to geology professor Shawn Willsey, a cluster of shield volcanoes several million years ago gave birth to basalt lava that periodically spread into the drainage and cooled. These blockages forced the creek to change course and seek a new path of least resistance on several occasions and in different locations. Salmon Butte, rising less than a mile from the current man-made dam, took its turn to pour lava into one of those ancient canyons. That hardened mass pushed the creek into its current pathway. The continual flow of the stream, enhanced at times by glacial torrents from the Jarbidge Mountains, then eroded down through the stacked basalt to create the vertical channel seen today.

As the nineteenth century came to a close, humans began eyeing the narrow chasm and brainstorming about creating their own diversion. The construction of Salmon Dam from 1908 to 1911 followed the design of A. J. Wiley, an engineer from Boise who had a far-reaching reputation as a dam builder. Prior to the relatively small structure that backed up Salmon Falls Creek, he helped design both the Swan Falls and Milner Dams on the Snake River. Afterwards he even played a role in the construction of Boulder Dam in Colorado and assisted on projects in Asia.

The construction that followed Wiley's plan took longer than anticipated, but the final product was an impressive 220-foot-high structure. While the concrete was poured, contractors worked on the outlet canal's two underground tunnels, a deep cut between them, and the many miles of downstream feeder canals and laterals. While some machinery could be powered by steam engines and electricity that had been brought to the site, much of the work was accomplished by men and horses. According to the 1910 Census, 60 percent of the 453 people involved in the project's construction were immigrants from mostly European countries. Fifteen different foreign languages were spoken.

It turned out that the initial planning for the project, as well as the actual water delivery, was less upfront and more complicated than the construction phase. The venture was one of many Carey Act projects that sought to bring irrigation water to the dry landscapes of the West. While the Homestead Act of 1862 and subsequent reforms enabled the federal government to bring settlers to the country's frontier, the legislation proved most practical on ground east of the 100th meridian. That region received enough rainfall during most seasons for individual farmers to grow harvestable crops. On the other side of that line that bisects Kansas, Nebraska, and the Dakotas, settlers had to find a way to pull water out of creeks and rivers. With that complication the act of farming demanded more than an independent nature and strong will. Irrigation systems made of substantial infrastructure usually required help from investors and some sort of government assistance.

Political leaders and both federal and state officials, concerned about the West's lack of settlement late in the nineteenth century, pointed to water as the answer. The concept of conservation came with a new twist: not consuming the resource actually meant wasting it. Leaders saw water as the foundation for economic policy, and the idea that arid lands needed to be "reclaimed" became popular. With the passage of the Carey Act in 1894 came the authority to release up to one million acres of federal land to each state. Those entities could then make their allotment available to private developers and financiers who would oversee the construction of dams and irrigation networks. Once irrigation water was delivered, the developers could recoup their investment by selling the land with its entitled water right to interested farmers.

Idaho utilized the Carey Act more than any of the western states, and little doubt exists that it successfully lured emigrants. Over a twenty-year period beginning in 1895, Idaho's population grew from 88,600 to 326,000—an increase nearly unmatched by any state. The success of individual projects, however, varied widely due to the conversion process that was often affected by dubious promotion, land speculation, and little oversight by state government. North of what eventually became known as the Salmon Tract, water from the Snake River had already been diverted via a project known as the Twin Falls South Side. While putting that system together had its own share of difficulties and growing pains, the Twin Falls Canal Company's endeavor became the most successful Carey Act project anywhere.

The development of land irrigated by Salmon Falls Creek, however, was fraught with major issues from the onset. In 1907 an initial estimate that the creek could irrigate close to 150,000 acres was confirmed by the Idaho State Engineer. Investor William Kuhn of the American Water Works and Guarantee Company of Pittsburgh, whose engineers had surveyed the drainage, readily agreed. The Idaho State Land Board soon approved the developer's plan but reduced the project to around 128,000 acres.

Kuhn organized the Twin Falls–Salmon River Land and Water Company—calling it a "creek" would not sound as appealing and many locals already referred to it as a river—and the promotion and selling of bonds on the national market commenced. Three million dollars were soon raised to fund the damming of the creek and the construction of the downstream delivery system. Looking forward to an optimistic future, the state land board bent the Carey Act's laws and ignored its own policies by allowing Kuhn to make the first 80,000 acres of land available to prospective farmers before irrigation water could be delivered.

The land lottery, originally planned on the Salmon Tract but instead held in Twin Falls in June of 1908, drew a crowd composed partly of unhappy land seekers. Those who had visited the project area earlier only to find a sea of sagebrush were appalled at the sight. Men who voiced unfavorable opinions about Kuhn and his backers prior to the lottery were verbally attacked. One critic intent on passing out handbills that accused the Salmon River Company of fraud was reportedly subdued by a company agent in a fistfight. While nearly all of the acreage available that day was accepted, many cautious land seekers began to view Kuhn and his company, along with the project, with concern.

Others held on to the assurance that water would be available within two years and began to clear sagebrush. Not until 1911 did the water begin to flow, but only 6,000 acres were irrigated. That amount rose to around 19,000 the next year, but even during the project's official celebration on June 28, it was apparent to everyone that something was wrong. Where was all the water that had been promised? The reservoir was not even close to full, and by early August deliveries ended. Complaints began working their way into the legal system. During that same year the Idaho Supreme Court ruled, much to the chagrin of farmers, that the canal company could indeed use a rotational delivery schedule "if necessity and the economical use of water required it." Realizing that they were in a battle over the delivery of sufficient water for the amount of land pledged, farmers organized into the 340-member Salmon River Settler's Association.

After the Kuhn empire entered bankruptcy in 1913 back in Pennsylvania, the canal company's financial situation was severely weakened. At the same time, court action between that entity's bondholders and farmers escalated. In addition to the judicial system, both the state land board and the federal government were forced to enter into the fray. The discontent continued for many years. In 1921 the last of the court cases was settled and the U.S. Department of the Interior issued a conclusive ruling. Only 35,000 acres would receive water on the Salmon Tract.

Why did less than one-fourth of the original prediction get irrigated? Overestimating the amount of water supply was a common practice across the West, whether for a Carey Act project or through other ventures. Little accountability from financiers and investors was required. And not only did the states fail to provide much oversight, but often their cheerleading role prevented them from questioning how much water a drainage would yield.

The Salmon Tract project, however, suffered from more than inflated forecasts. In 1969 the U.S. Geological Survey studied historic data regarding the amount of water that flowed into and out of the reservoir. Those statistics were sobering for anyone trying to grow crops on the Salmon Tract. While an average of 107,000 acre-feet reached the reservoir, only 75,000 actually entered the delivery system. What happened to the rest? Estimates were made that 20,000 seeped out from the reservoir while another 6,000 evaporated from it. Five thousand acre-feet leaked around the dam through the basalt lava flows and then dropped back down to the creek. The final 1,000 were redelivered back into two small drainages that added to the reservoir's total from upstream.

The numbers don't become any more favorable once the water flowed into the canals. While there is no way to prevent a certain amount of leakage through any irrigation lateral constructed with earthen embankments, stretches of canals and laterals underlain by porous lava rock helped push the loss rate up to over 40 percent for the delivery system.

While much of that data came from a twenty-year period beginning in the late 1930s, and some of the most porous sections were tackled during that time, the efficiency issue continues to be addressed. The Salmon River Canal Company annually utilizes a portion of its water assessment fees for conservation projects. The most porous stretches of some of the larger canals have been lined with textile fabric, and other smaller waterways have been replaced by pipelines. Many farmers have invested in pressurized irrigation systems—mostly center pivots—that enable them to utilize their precious resource more efficiently. And it's obvious that Salmon Tract farmers have a different mentality when it comes to water—I get a feel for that each time I get to work with them on irrigation projects. They see that liquid as a more finite resource than those who farm—or like me, who once farmed—on the Twin Falls tract. With water from the Snake River, we hold a high expectation to irrigate all our land and grow any crop we choose. We can get away with some inefficiency and not have it come back to haunt us.

Salmon Tract irrigators don't have that luxury. They're quick to discuss the latest snowfall totals in the higher country, listen carefully to projected stream flow reports, and plant their crops—or in some cases not seed certain fields or specific crops—based on the water forecast. None of their prized commodity leaves the tract. And even with all that fretting and conservation, during some seasons they can still run out of water by July or August. While dealing with that degree of uncertainty seems to have made those left on the tract both practical and resilient, they seem to remain an optimistic bunch.

Did that desire to conserve everything that enters the reservoir and delivery system contribute to a minor disaster in 1984? The snow survey supervisor of the Soil Conservation Service was quoted in a *New York Times* article in January of that year as describing southern Idaho's snowpack as "extreme." The Salmon Falls Creek reservoir was predicted to likely fill for the first time. Near perfect conditions that maximized the melt-off that spring then sent a massive volume of water toward the dam's impoundment. While downstream landowners expressed concern in April about the potential inflow, the Salmon River Canal Company decided not to release any water until the reservoir level was five feet below capacity.

On May 11 that level was reached and around 400 cubic feet per second (cfs) were spilled into the canyon. Three days later, with the reservoir still rising, the flow increased to almost 1,000 cfs—fifty times the average leakage from the dam. The day after that the earthen fill at Balanced Rock Crossing gave way when it became saturated due to a large pool that was created when the single ten-foot steel culvert could not carry the incoming water. An unimaginable flow—estimated at 7,500 cfs—then raced downstream and destroyed irrigation pumping stations used to supply the Magic Water tract. Property and homes near the mouth of the creek were also damaged by the flood.

Those affected by the deluge filed a lawsuit against the canal company, which denied it was responsible for flood control and claimed the two highway districts that maintained the road crossing were at fault. In 1988 a jury found that the canal company did have a duty for flood control and that they were 40 percent liable. The highway departments were assessed the same share of responsibility, while the downstream interests were given the remaining 20 percent. Three years later the Idaho Supreme Court overturned that ruling and freed the canal company of the flood control obligation. It decided, however, that the Salmon River Canal Company could be held liable for its actions and was expected to act reasonably when releasing water. The second trial in 1993 resulted in a decision that the water-delivery entity alone was responsible. The amount of damages was set at $2 million plus nearly nine years of interest.

Faced with having to pay $4 million and without the assets to do so, the canal company declared bankruptcy. Discussions were held between the company's board of directors and its stockholders—those irrigators possessing shares—and proposals were voted on. Settlement offers were then made to those parties affected downstream. The negotiations ended when a $2.2 million check was delivered to the plaintiffs. The outcome spread a substantial financial burden over the 174 stockholders who as a group, in part due to two very poor water years, were unable to secure financing for the payment.

With one last look back at the dam before resuming our downstream jaunt, I ponder the challenges of the Salmon Tract and humanity's management of water. In the early twentieth century, long before the surge of environmental regulations of the 1970s, little thought was given to completely dewatering a stream corridor. Loss of habitat for fish and wildlife, the drying up of valuable wetlands, and damage to a landscape's beauty were attributes often given little priority. Controlling the West's water meant controlling the land. Progress and growth and utilizing God's resources to the fullest were priorities to be aggressively pursued. The prevailing attitude ensured that sacrifices needed to be made for the good of the country and an individual's right to prosper.

On most irrigation projects during that era, the plan called for diverting as much water as possible—even all of it. When Salmon Dam started to block the natural flow of water and the reservoir began to fill, I can only guess that most people were thrilled at the sight. When the water rose high enough and found a seam in the lava flows that allowed it to seep around man's impervious construction, I can also imagine their surprise and disappointment. As an irrigator of many decades and someone who still owns and lives on a farm that requires water, I can feel their pain.

But another part of me is grateful for the liquid that will not be contained and either leaks around each side of the dam or, in the case of the east wall of the canyon, springs out from between a pair of basalt flows and returns to the stream channel. That point of view is selfish—I cannot deny that. I have enjoyed many hunting and fishing trips and certainly have an emotional tie with the water in the bottom of the canyon. But the thought of drying up twenty-five miles of creek to Lilly Grade and devastating an ecosystem where fish from the ocean once swam seems like a heavy price to pay.

About a half mile below the dam, Beth and I look across the canyon to see the scar left from the 1984 emergency release. As the dam itself had no means to spill excess water, the opening to the second tunnel was closed and the canal breached just upstream. With the flow diverted to the west, it then poured over the canyon's inner ledge and created a 120-foot waterfall. The sight must have been both exciting and disconcerting.

After we follow the next bend in the canyon, we again find ourselves in a wild environment that provokes no thoughts of man, irrigation, or floods. We proceed another mile along the inner rim before the bench ends and we are forced to climb completely out of the canyon. On top the wind greets us with its full force, but its effect seems minimal since little remains of our hike.

Within a quarter mile we leave the canyon for good when a deep ravine once fed by the diverted Antelope Springs guides us to the west and eventually to our pickup. We agree that the short hike was just what we needed and discuss the next segment as we drive away.

In another week we hope to return to this same spot, but only after a hike along one of the most remote and untouched stretches of canyon that Salmon Falls Creek offers.

The remains of a fogbank drift inside the canyon at Lilly Grade.

Balanced Rock steals the show among a collection of rhyolite pillars.

A trickle of water runs down the Snake River's north channel at Upper Salmon Falls.

After separating from the rim, a block of land (top center) sinks and crowds the downslope terrain, which then rotates up into the creek. The dam backs up water for a mile.

Beth Cothern walks into the canyon upstream of the county park at Balanced Rock.

The canyon near Lilly Grade exhibits a classic V-shape as the creek erodes through horizontal basalt lava flows.

A group of men pose for the camera at Salmon Dam two years after its completion. Courtesy of Twin Falls Public Library. Salmon Dam_679 by Clarence Bisbee.

The creek winds through a shallow canyon before emptying into the irrigation reservoir.

An assortment of boulders and formations are found scattered across the Granite Range.

The creek remains hidden as it navigates the broken landscape of the Bad Lands.

Camp Creek shapes its own scenic canyon while escaping from the high country.

Five peaks stand in line on the north end of the Jarbidge Mountains

Chapter 10

APRIL 19–20

After postponing our twenty-mile trip and settling instead on the short stretch of canyon below Salmon Dam, Beth and I return to Lilly Grade a week later. As our son again drops us off, I feel a twinge of failure over not meeting one of my few rules of engagement for this year's adventure. Starting the next outing where the previous one ended did not seem like it would be that difficult. But now here we are, I think, putting a couple of pieces to this landscape puzzle together out of order.

The hiccup really shouldn't matter, but it runs counter to my often linear manner of taking on the world. After a few minutes, however, the rhythm of walking returns me to the present and the thoughts of foiled plans vanish. The change in strategy also serves as a reminder about the approach required for any outdoor endeavor. One must accept and adapt to what the land and weather sometimes combine to offer.

Since I had not bothered to retrieve the camping gear cached a week earlier, we are still free to carry daypacks. In addition, most of the hike will be along the rim since it will be almost impossible to scramble through this next stretch of canyon like we did between the main crossings. Except for the first few miles upstream from the grade where I hunted ducks with my father and later ventured solo, the acute V-shape of the gorge thwarts much foot travel.

And that is not just my take on the canyon. In 1975 an archaeological review, led by Gordon Tucker, was undertaken by Idaho State University to meet the Bureau of Land Management's need to inventory the canyon upstream from Balanced Rock. While the original plan called for searching the depths of the canyon and along each rim, little surveying was done inside the chasm upstream from the grade. The final report observed that "the bottom became increasingly more boulder-choked the farther upstream we went and that the number of sites became more scarce."

A few minutes after starting, we edge close to the rim and peer directly down at Lilly Grade's asphalt. The perspective fascinates me. I have viewed this road cut on dozens of occasions from either down by the creek or along the opposite rim, and driven it more times than I can remember. This morning is the first time, however, that I have stood over it.

A hundred years ago, in an attempt to find a shorter route between the Magic Valley and the booming mining camp of Jarbidge, some seventy-five miles away, discussions began on improving what was then known as the "Lilly Trail." With the town of Buhl hoping to benefit from the increase in traffic, their highway district committed to constructing a functional road on the east side of the creek, with the county being responsible for the opposite side. Since then frequent maintenance work and multiple widening projects took place. The entire two miles of road surface was not completely paved until the late 1990s.

Within an hour the crossing and civilization lay behind us, but evidence of the land's original inhabitants materializes in the form of a partial arrowhead that I nearly step on. Black in color but not as glassy as obsidian, the ignimbrite flake makes for a pleasant surprise. Its presence also reminds me that there is nothing novel about walking the edge of the canyon—humans have been doing it for thousands of years. While Beth and I are here for enjoyment and those archaeology students examined the ground to gain knowledge, the native people connected to this weapon needed to live off this landscape as they passed through.

After rubbing the artifact between my thumb and forefinger and giving it one last inspection, I return the tool to its resting place underneath a small clump of sagebrush. The piece, I assume, was missed by Tucker and his crew. Items found having diagnostic value, like this one, were collected and taken to Pocatello to be studied and compared to similar findings elsewhere in the Great Basin–Columbia Plateau region. With the age of those known sites already determined through radiocarbon dating, the researchers tried to piece together the story of how and when the people inhabited this country.

Four decades ago Tucker theorized that aboriginal people were present along the drainage as far back as nine thousand years ago. After finding more handcrafted projectile points and source material above the canyon's west rim than its east, he concluded that the native people's presence there was greater than where Beth and I walk. He also questioned ethnographer Julian Steward's theory about most foot travel occurring from the Snake River to the uplands and back again. Tucker believed that those seasonal rounds only took place in the recent past and primarily when fish were in short supply.

When I asked Kelly Murphy to help me sort out some of the dynamics, he said that after Tucker's work the accepted view settled on native presence going back to at least 10,800 years ago. That the west side of the canyon was more frequently used is almost certain, and likely because the two main tributaries on the lower end of the Salmon Falls drainage enter from that direction. The smaller canyons created by Devil Creek, where Beth and I camped, and Cedar Creek, which we will soon see, contained accessible water and nutrition in a way that the big, deep fissure did not. A very short drainage near Salmon Dam, birthed by Antelope Springs, also originates from the west and would have been an additional area where the nomads likely lingered.

As far as who came from where, it seems Native Americans began their seasonal rounds from both directions. Some Snake River residents certainly headed south to the uplands and returned in the fall.

Other Shoshone bands from present-day Utah and Nevada headed down-country in the opposite direction to fish and trade with those who stayed along the river. Kelly surmised that for those families wanting to move in the quickest, most efficient manner, there were two choices: stay on the east side where no tributary canyons got in the way or bypass much of Salmon Falls and follow Devil Creek. Regardless of the direction or side of Salmon Falls the people frequented, Kelly agreed with both Tucker and Steward that the prey most often sought was smaller game. Not only were these animals most likely to be found along the canyon, but trying to pin an antelope or deer against the rim usually took more than just one extended family to result in a successful hunt.

My chance encounter with the artifact makes me wonder about its story—from the volcanic forces that created the source rock to the human artistry that shaped it into a weapon. Those visions along with its final flight swirl around in my mind and mix with the immediate landscape. Conjured up in the present by touching the past, these kind of experiences are as close as I ever get to time travel. And standing here on the rim of this deep canyon helps prolong the sensation.

But even today there is no escaping that these moments don't last long. With the glimpse of a distant power line when we turn around to resume our journey, the illusion begins to fall apart. I look down quickly as if searching and finding another arrowhead will delay the inevitable, but it's too late. The spell is broken and I return to the present, but find it not such a bad place to be either.

Because of the distinctive geology and scenery, along with its nearly untouched state between the two rims, the BLM classified this stretch of canyon as a Wilderness Study Area several decades ago. Other recognition includes an Area of Critical Environmental Concern designation and potential for Wild and Scenic River status. But Beth and I don't see the drainage in terms of the labels and accolades bestowed upon it. Nor do we give much thought to the fact that for most of the morning our position along the canyon places us no more than four miles from our home. Little else seems to matter other than the sight of the canyon, the soft rush of the creek at the bottom, and the solitude. On this calm morning we just walk the rim and lose ourselves.

Our satisfying connection with the earth and the jagged cut across its surface is eventually interrupted midway through the day's journey. Our destination for the night lies on the other side of the canyon, and we have arrived at the only place I know to cross. We must drop down into the canyon's depths where we will experience wilderness firsthand and get the chance to confirm the rationale for all the categorical praise. When I remind Beth about our need to descend, her reaction comes as no surprise. I knew when and where this traverse would occur. She did not.

"Here? Down this steep part?"

I try to sound confident. "Yes. I have gone down twice before and up the other side once with a full pack. Our camping gear is on the other side of the canyon, farther upstream, so we have to cross. We'll be fine."

Our conversation about the slope continues for a few minutes and then veers off into the question of safety and potential consequences of me going to places like this alone. After that the topic peters out, mostly because I have little to contribute, and there is nothing left to do but begin our plunge. For most of the way down we grab onto one sagebrush plant at a time or whatever else might help apply the brakes to a shift in momentum that can come quickly.

After we reach the bottom and cross the creek where a pile of boulders nearly fills the channel, we push upstream. With no trail to follow, our path of least resistance takes us through the typical combination of brush, junipers, and talus set on a steep side slope that often dives right into the stream. After a half mile of bushwhacking through the mess, which includes a new foe in the form of budding poison ivy plants, we reach the mouth of another chasm entering from the south. I tell Beth that this gorge cut by Cedar Creek is the reason we started on the opposite side of Salmon Falls—otherwise a significant detour around the tributary canyon would have been required. She doesn't seem convinced, and after considering the effort spent inside this nearly impassable abyss, I also question my logic.

Before the climb out we eat lunch and rest in a rare flat area formed by the shared floodplain of the two creeks. On my previous visit here I took time to fish the creek and caught several small redband, a subspecies of rainbow trout. Since the native fish generally require cold, free-flowing water, their existence in southern Idaho is generally confined to a high-desert environment on the edge of or away from civilization.

Thoughts of the diminutive native give way to the consideration of other endemic species, these much bigger, that might have graced these waters. Earlier when noticing the stream channel in spots was filled with rocks that had broken off from the rim that we stood over, I had wondered about the salmon and steelhead. Did they make it past those boulder piles, some of which might be a hundred feet in length? No physical evidence of anadromous fish exists above Balanced Rock, twenty miles downstream, but then again, fish bone doesn't preserve well. And while the rock piles look impassable now, the higher spring and early-summer flows fed by snowmelt before the dam was built would have made those obstacles more navigable.

The contemplation on those iconic creatures working their way upstream doesn't last much longer than it takes to eat our lunch. Having been inside the canyon longer than anticipated, we do not have the luxury of lingering. By the time we complete our exit, the time spent negotiating a single mile inside the gorge will almost equal the half-dozen miles that preceded it. Our immediate surroundings have also begun to make me a little nervous about another cold-blooded animal on this warm April day. The tangle of shrubs and rocks and tall grass we stumbled through and that still surround us seems like good rattlesnake habitat. Or perhaps it's just a small dose of claustrophobia seeping through my arteries. Regardless of my anxiety's source, I'm thankful when we feel rested enough to begin the climb out.

On the way up I attempt to reassure both of us about having once found a route through the several flows of basalt stacked along the rim. While the entire four hundred feet of elevation gain challenges our hearts and lungs, it's the last fifty that tests my resolve. The cliffs seem taller and more formidable than when encountered five years earlier, but my unease is soon tempered by Beth's lead. She climbs up through the final, and steepest, rock face with ease and then offers moral support and a helping hand. I am grateful for her presence and acknowledge that this is the second time in two months that I have benefitted from her calm and skill.

Standing on flat, stony ground between the canyons cut by Salmon Falls and Cedar Creeks allows us to take a deep breath. Our placement on the outside bend of the main canyon also treats us to an incredible panorama. A pair of rocks provides a place to sit and enjoy our reward, but we don't have much time to idle. We resume our hike along the rim, still in awe but now with much more respect for the wild landscape below.

After a mile a deep ravine enters the canyon and deflects us from the day's companion, but we need to angle off in a new direction anyway. Somewhere near the head of this tributary fissure lies a faint two-track I drove once that will lead us to our camping gear. Within a half hour we find and begin following the route that parallels our now hidden canyon. Neither one of us cares much about its disappearance, however, since we are both to the point that we want the walking to end. Not that I have much to complain about—Beth is the one whose feet have grown another crop of blisters. Our walk proceeds in silence until we reach our destination an hour before sundown.

While a mile away from the canyon in a nondescript location, the spot has a significant pull on me. I drive here several times each spring to count sage-grouse that have gathered in a small clearing surrounded by sagebrush. Typically over two-dozen male birds, performing an annual ritual driven by reproduction, put on a fascinating show in this open space called a lek.

The core of the bird's display consists of inflating a pair of yellow airs sacs, normally hidden by feathers on either side of their throat, to the size of small balloons. The sudden deflation then creates a "boop" sound that cannot be confused with anything else heard out here in the sage steppe. At the same time the males, which weigh around seven pounds, fan out their tail feathers and strut. The "Hey, look at me!" posturing attempts to intimidate birds of the same sex and attract those of the opposite. On this particular lek the flock spreads out for a hundred yards, with the younger birds hanging around the perimeter and the older males defending prime territory in the center. While the gathering is mostly about looks, rival males sometimes do more than just face off and attempt to strike each other with a flurry of wing flaps.

A hen might spend several days along the edge of the clearing sizing up the prospects before venturing onto the lek to make her choice. The reproductive act itself is then over in an instant. With studies having shown that only 10 percent of the males do almost all the breeding, only a few birds on this lek will be successful. The rest of the flock? They seem to have no choice but to follow their instinct and show up well before sunrise, regardless of the prospect of failure, and perform for several hours from early March into May. And while this commitment during the spring is required for the survival of the species, it is also the most dangerous phase in their life cycle. While several kinds of predators might take advantage of their vulnerability, getting picked off by an eagle represents the biggest threat to the distracted dancers. At this location where a golden eagle coming from the canyon might only be a few minutes away, the level of peril is likely greater.

After leaving the lek a bred female chooses a site within a few miles amidst an expanse of sagebrush where she can nest underneath one of the shrubs. While adults feed mostly on the leaves of the plant, and in the winter exclusively on them, chicks must first feast on insects drawn to a vegetative mix that includes wildflowers and native bunchgrasses. The set of integrated habitats required to support the different stages of its life cycle gives the iconic bird an even greater stature. The sage-grouse is often referred to as an umbrella species, meaning that other wildlife also benefit from the presence of a healthy landscape that it occupies. Smaller birds like the sage thrasher and sagebrush sparrow, along with mammals ranging from the pygmy rabbit to pronghorn antelope, all require sagebrush and thrive when its presence is in balance with other vegetation.

Over the last four decades, however, the population of sage-grouse has suffered a 90 percent reduction in the twelve western states where it lives. The species has been a candidate for listing under the Endangered Species Act, and its presence is a driving force for the management of public lands possessing sage-steppe ecosystems. While causes of its decline may include predation, West Nile virus, and human activities and infrastructure, the central issue seems to be loss of quality habitat. The main culprit for that decline in southern Idaho is easy to guess. The unprecedented large wildfires over the last fifteen years—many of them well over a hundred thousand acres—have been devastating to the species.

In addition to working for the Natural Resources Conservation Service with ranchers on occasional projects that will benefit both livestock and sage-grouse, about ten years ago I jumped at the chance to go search for the birds. Idaho Fish and Game needed volunteers to find the species' dancing grounds not visited for a few years and make counts that help estimate population trends. Armed with a GPS unit, a map, and binoculars, I became hooked. After several seasons of looking for random leks, the agency assigned a specific set of locations for me to visit four times each spring. And on that route I became enamored with this spot where I could watch birds perform less than fifty yards away from my parked truck.

Beth has only seen displaying birds elsewhere from a much greater distance. I thought that since this spot was near the halfway point of our weekend hike, it would serve as a nice bonus to our trip. Of all the performance venues on my route and others that I have visited, this lek is at the top of my list. The viewing is not hampered by vegetation or topography, and the birds seem to care little about my presence.

After retrieving our camping gear left cached in the sagebrush, I set up our small tent a safe distance away and below the sightline of the birds that will gather the next morning. As dusk begins to settle over the desert plain, I hear the familiar sound of a couple of sage-grouse popping their air sacs. Apparently some birds just cannot wait to start the party. Not wanting to take a chance at disturbing them, we remain in the tent and listen. While the evening activity is short-lived, the birds wake me several hours before sunrise when a few again sound off under a waning moon. I look forward to dawn and the chance to see birds.

But as the sky begins to lighten, I realize that I have miscalculated. Between yesterday's trying hike, the hard ground, and her blistered feet, Beth has had a miserable night. When the time comes to view our feathered neighbors, she gamely takes a look, but I can see her heart just isn't into it. The magic that I had hoped to find fails to materialize, having been overwhelmed by the result of the previous day's journey. In my preoccupation to share the experience of the lek with her, I overlooked the cost of getting here.

When we take a close look at Beth's feet, smaller blisters seem to have grown inside some of the multiple original offenders. I find the sight hard to fathom, but after devoting a considerable amount of time tending to her feet, she announces her desire to start walking. We take one last look at the birds, sneak away from the lek, and angle back to the canyon. When we return to the rim several miles upstream from where we left, the drop to the creek seems farther than ever. I wonder if my mind is playing tricks on me, but a study of my map confirms the observation. The stacked contour lines add up to nearly six hundred feet, which is half again as deep as most of this canyon that I have come to know.

The rocky grandeur of this crevice carved by Salmon Falls Creek in some ways makes it feel like a solid, stable piece of terrain. But words of wisdom echoing through my head, again provided by geology professor Willsey, remind me that permanence is not the case. Whether it was the glacial melt from Nevada from several ice ages that contributed to create the canyon's present state or the lava flows from shield volcanoes that periodically rerouted the drainages, there has been little long-term stability to this landscape. And back before Salmon Falls Creek even existed, southern Idaho streams actually flowed into Nevada. It wasn't until the tectonic plate that we ride on passed over the hot spot now under Yellowstone, and contributed to the formation of a lowered Snake River Plain, that drainages flowed in the current direction.

The lesson on transformation prompts me to think about the future. If I was able enough to come back here in another quarter century and look down from this same perspective, could I see a shift to something else? Likely not, since the earth's processes rarely occur as quickly as an event like Sinking Canyon forty miles downstream. But that does not mean nothing is happening.

By mid-afternoon we choose to ignore a bend in the canyon and instead head straight toward our truck. Before committing to the shortcut's last few miles, one final pause seems in order. While Beth removes her shoes and cools her blisters, I hike a few hundred yards toward a small rise that will enable me to soak up one final view of Salmon Falls Creek and its monumental cut. After finding the best spot to see the canyon in both directions, I consider the future oversight of this stretch of canyon. Because of its proximity to a network of two-track roads, the creek's restricted flow due to the dam, and the limited access inside the gorge, the BLM recommended that the area not receive a wilderness designation. Policy ensures that the corridor be managed to preserve its wild condition, however, until legislation passed by Congress either declares it formal wilderness or releases it for multiple use.

Soon after beginning a different route back down to my wife, I stumble upon a lithic scatter composed of several dozen pieces of black and brown stone flakes. What went through the minds of the natives who might have paused on this same rise? What did the artisan see who sat here and reduced fist-sized rocks into something more usable? While his or her people also might have referred to this canyon in several different ways, notions about possession and control, at least before the Euro-Americans came, likely did not cross their minds.

The connection to and meaning derived from this landscape is something that I likely cannot begin to fathom. I have read that sage-grouse, for example, were utilized by Native Americans as a food source and assume that the birds were most easily taken when occupying a lek. A few tribes were inspired enough by the spring ritual that they included some of the grouse's moves into their own dance. What else might have linked the bird and people together? I have no idea.

But I can, mixed in with musings of past and future use, take stock of my present relationship with this canyon. Regardless of what label might be attached to this remote country, passing through it and bearing witness to such a stunning landmark has been both evocative and humbling.

Chapter 11

MAY 24

For the first time since February, the next venture begins without my wife. After finishing our latest march with blisters that totaled into the double digits, Beth decided that she was done hiking for a while. While she had tried many combinations of shoes and socks over the last several months, nothing had seemed to work very well. And although she had not committed to the entire project, I miss her company and wonder if I could have planned better. Did we try to cover too much ground over that last trip? Should we have split the hike up into smaller portions and tackled them one day at a time? Would her feet have blistered anyway?

Since it's impossible to know the outcome from any changes made, I suppose the second-guessing does not accomplish much. As our progress pulled us farther away from home, the logistics of each trip naturally became more complicated. Our last trip required four hours of driving time that included delivering gear into the middle of nowhere so as to lighten our loads over the hike that covered almost twenty-five miles. To make it to the top of the Jarbidge Mountains from this point forward, close to that length needs to be walked each month. The amount doesn't sound like much, but consuming it in smaller bites would require more trips, driving, other people's time, and days to steal off the calendar.

Eventually I recognize the need to quit with the analysis and just walk. My plan for the first day of Memorial Day weekend consists of a fifteen-mile hike beginning at Salmon Dam. I park on the east side of the cemented construction so something new can be experienced—walking across the top of it. After starting across the curved route, I first hear and then see a truck approaching from behind. While the passage atop the dam is too narrow for a pair of automobiles to pass, there is room for a single vehicle and one pedestrian to share its width. Since I am the one on foot, however, I cannot help but jam my body against the crumbled sidewall to make sure there is plenty of separation between us.

Already leaning over the three-foot-high barrier, I peer down into the placid water backed up by the mass of concrete. A few steps across the pavement then allow me to gauge the severe downstream drop and observe the water leaking around both sides of the dam. With no more traffic to contend with, I make several more comparisons while taking a zigzag route across the perched roadway. After the game ends at the other side of the dam, I follow the pavement to the top of the canyon's upper rim.

From that vantage point I look across the reservoir to Lud Drexler Park and am astounded to see what looks like a small town composed of at least fifty recreational camping vehicles, several tents, and a large number of pickups and boat trailers. Having always intended to walk on the west side of the reservoir, I am thankful for not having to navigate through or around the mass of holiday humanity.

The conventional practice of walking the rim commences, but now instead of peering down into the bottom of a canyon, the void is filled with water. The calm fluid that reflects the blue sky is periodically broken by a boat that creates a white V as it leaves the edge of the park and begins its charge up the fifteen-mile-long reservoir. The impounded water is an angler's paradise that holds a variety of species that includes rainbow trout—southern Idaho's most common species—and bass, perch, and the best walleye fishing in the state. Since the reservoir's outlet is a hundred feet above the dam's base, even the most severe drought, while offering little to farmers, does not draw the water level down enough to adversely affect most fish.

What captures my imagination, however, has little to do with the boaters, their destinations on the reservoir, or the fish swimming in its depths. I instead try to stare down through the water as if I could see the bottom of the Salmon Falls Creek drainage before the dam was built and the landscape flooded. The topography of the canyon here was vastly different than the deep, imposing chasm that Beth and I had either walked along or hiked through for the last sixty miles. In this stretch the canyon was wider, shallower, and in many places without much of a rim. A meandering Salmon Falls Creek passed through a corridor of willow groves in the midst of a landscape that grew enough grass to sustain a handful of small ranches and their homesteads.

Wallace Stegner once wrote, "The names contain our history as the seed contains the tree." My map not only pays tribute to those people who once lived near the creek but sometimes hints of actual events. Gray's Landing. Norton Bay. Whiskey Slough. At the age of thirteen Thomas Ike Gray—whose stories were compiled by family member Karen Quinton in her book *Life in the Saddle on the South Idaho Desert*—moved with his family to Salmon Falls "River" in 1890. After several years his father and other settlers began filing paperwork for land patents obtained through the Desert Land Act. Passed in 1877, the amendment to the Homestead Act served as an attempt to adapt to the arid, less-productive West. Settlers paid fifty cents for each acre filed on and were required to reclaim the land by irrigating and cultivating it within three years. After offering proof of their efforts and paying another one dollar per acre, they could then claim ownership.

The first edition of the Desert Land Act, however, was fraught with abuse. Intended to promote the establishment of individual farms, it was backed and utilized often by wealthy cattlemen. A common practice that circumvented the intent of the program involved having large ranch businesses acquire land that their employees first filed on and obtained. A temporary suspension of the program and subsequent reforms in 1891 restricted the total acreage that any one person could acquire through all available programs to 320 acres, or double that for a married couple. After other safeguards were enacted, a wave of applications again began to be processed.

In 1894 Thomas McBeth Gray filed on land several miles upstream from where I stand. The following year A. D. Norton submitted paperwork at the Land Office in Hailey on a spot two miles away, making his place the nearest to that of the Grays. At least a half dozen other tracts along the drainage were converted to private property during the decade. While it was hoped the latest version of the Desert Land Act would better promote settlement by homesteading families, it too was still utilized by large operations. Nora Sparks, whose husband was the founder of the Sparks-Harral ranching empire and a future governor of Nevada, acquired a half-section on the reservoir's upper end at China Creek.

What was life on the homestead like for the Grays? Quinton believes that it must have been a tough, isolating experience, but the family did build a sustainable operation. Instead of concentrating on cattle, they focused on the raising of Percheron horses, whose ability to pull heavy wagons and farm equipment made them the most popular horse breed in the country at the turn of the century. According to son Thomas Ike in *Life in the Saddle*, the Gray family eventually built up a herd of over one hundred animals.

A few crops were grown on the farm, and when Thomas McBeth began raising grain to sell as livestock feed, the family obtained the Salmon River country's first threshing machine. And while the motive for the family's move was certainly due to the water, its value went beyond irrigation and drinking water for both humans and livestock. Quinton points out that the mother of the clan, Susan, who had grown up in the Clearwater River country of northern Idaho and was a member of the Nez Perce tribe, loved to fish for salmon and wanted to be near a decent stream.

The Gray family's existence on their homestead began to crumble when Thomas McBeth died of cancer in 1900 and was buried at the ranch. Some of the family persisted there for a few years, but by the time construction began on Salmon Dam in 1908, all of the land that would be flooded by the reservoir had been purchased by the Twin Falls–Salmon River Land and Water Company. The remains of Thomas and daughter Mae were reinterred thirty miles away at the Twin Falls Cemetery before their not-so-final resting places were inundated.

Contemplating the area's former residents keeps me loyal to the transformed creek, but several forces compel me to veer off in another direction. The canyon has begun to lose its charm and at times reminds me of a half-full bathtub. Another factor comes in the form of a change in topography to the west. Having walked across the southern half of the relatively flat Snake River Plain, I am now in close proximity to steep terrain that rises only a few miles away—and I can feel its pull.

After circling around a flooded side canyon called Antelope Bay, I leave the reservoir behind. My new route angles through a belt of terrain that lies perched above the drainage and below the adjacent ridge. Named Browns Bench after the first settler who arrived to the region in the 1860s, the strip runs south for twenty miles.

My first destination on the bench is a spot that offered temporary shelter to the Native Americans who preceded those white settlers seeking permanence along Salmon Falls Creek. A collapsed lava tube labeled Indian Cave on the map contains an opening less than ten feet high and wide, but tunnels back underground a hundred feet. Located on state-managed land and easily accessible to the public from a worn two-track road, the cave has long since been scavenged of anything having cultural significance. I look for a pictograph seen inside the cave while on a tour several decades earlier. While my search comes up empty, the cavern's air temperature, easily ten degrees cooler than aboveground, offers a pleasant escape. I am also relieved at what is not found: the shelter seems to contain no sign of rattlesnakes known to occasionally seek out the cool, dark environment.

The cave is one of many sites on Browns Bench that provides evidence of native people. With Salmon Falls Creek no longer buried in the bottom of a deep canyon, and the nearby uplands offering an extra element of diversity, the nomads would have spent more time here than back to the north. A stone hunting blind near the base of the hills, a multitude of lithic scatters, and even a burial site found in the broken rimrock along the reservoir have all confirmed their presence.

An archaeologist from the Bureau of Land Management, Jeff Ross, once described the region to me as being seasonally inhabited by the Western Shoshone and as the outer range for other groups from the south. He pointed out that the landscape was rich in resources that the Indians needed for subsistence like seeds, roots, animals, and fish. In addition, the area was known as a key source for material used to create high-quality tools. The prevalence of and demand for the Browns Bench ignimbrite, or opaque obsidian, resulted in the locals trading it with other tribes. The sought-after stone has been found as far away as Texas.

After reluctantly leaving the cool oasis of the cave and stepping back underneath the sun, I continue my mostly southward bearing in hopes of finding more of the past. This time the hunt focuses on proof from a not-so-distant era. In the 1870s the Browns Bench corridor began serving as a temporary, yet crucial, shipping lane. Since the railroad companies had not yet laid all the lines that would fully connect the West, overland freighting remained vital to supplying growing communities. Southern Idaho offered at least four roads where oxen or mules pulled wagons loaded with supplies. One such route began from a Central Pacific Railroad stop at the now vanished town of Toano, Nevada. Two years after the Golden Spike was driven a hundred miles to the east, the "Toana" Road, as it eventually became known, started to transport freight to what was then called Boise City. In its heyday the "fast freight line" service could make the trip in a week. An additional selling point was the ability to backhaul feed and other goods to supply both the freight road's rest stations and the copper mining district in Contact, Nevada.

Before the road became functional, however, construction was needed to fortify stream crossings and to build grades in and out of several tributary canyons to Salmon Falls Creek. In addition, buildings were often erected at rest stations that were usually placed at least twelve miles apart and at spots where water and ample grass could be found. Many of the laborers were Chinese who began immigrating to the United States in the mid-1860s to work on the railroads.

When the last section of the Oregon Short Line Railroad was completed in 1884 and linked Pocatello to Boise, the need for the Toana and other freight roads ended. Evidence of the Toana Road remained, but the route itself was largely forgotten. I found out about it a couple of decades ago when my mother, while taking a class focusing on local history, researched the road for a paper she wrote. In 2003 and 2004, as part of a grant-funded project, Shawna and Zeke Robinson spent several hundred hours documenting the portion of the route from the Idaho-Nevada boundary to the Snake River. After their fieldwork was completed and another party had written up the report, the route was listed on the National Register of Historic Places.

Shortly after that formality, the Robinsons took me on a tour to look at a few spots along the Toana Road. We visited several of the rest stations and looked at some pristine road segments. We ended the day speculating on a set of three out-of-place rock piles that were rumored to be the burial sites of Chinese laborers who had been murdered. Regardless of what might have happened at that particular spot, the immigrants certainly were not always treated well—even after the construction of the West's railroads and other important infrastructure ended. Once their cheap labor was no longer needed and the mining industry saw them as competition, the Chinese Exclusion Act of 1882 prevented further immigration into the United States. That federal law was the first and only major legislation to openly stop immigration for a specific nationality. Ten years later the Geary Act continued the ban into the twentieth century.

Portions of the main gravel road that now runs the length of Browns Bench occupy the same footprint where the freight route was located. Armed with a map created from the Robinsons' exploration, I hunt for isolated segments off the beaten path. I find several spots that, while on occasion appear to be driven on by modern vehicles, look to be the real thing. Eventually I locate a rest station visited with the Robinsons and take a few minutes to explore the immediate area. Not much remains except for a few lines of rock that might have been a building foundation and some small fragments of glass and porcelain scattered around the site. It's not surprising that a few flakes of obsidian also turn up. Anyone who frequented the arid West was drawn to its accessible water, lush vegetation, and the increased concentration of wildlife found along those moist sites.

After leaving the rest station, I reconnect with and walk down the main road toward a spot harboring my own private source of water. Early that morning I cached a couple of frozen water bottles, and now the thought of sipping something ice cold while eating lunch sounds extravagant. Shortly after arriving at my destination, however, a ten-minute hunt through a patch of sagebrush not far from the road turns up empty. Even though I recall using a specific wood post in a fence that intersects the road as a reference point, it appears that my memory should not be trusted. Perhaps sketching out a map with an X that marked the spot of my coveted treasure would have been wiser. I also wonder about my need for hiding the plastic bottles. It's just water—even if mistaken for trash, would anyone have taken it? And while the holiday weekend might bring more traffic down the back road than usual, I have seen exactly one truck during the last two hours of walking on or near the main road.

I give up after another futile search is spent questioning both my sanity and need for secrecy. Before I have a chance to sit down, eat lunch, and mourn over having missed the chance to have cold water trickle down my throat, I spy a car coming down the road. My focus turns away from my missing water and toward my fellow travelers after seeing that the couple has noticed me and slowed down as they pass by. In an uncommon moment I feel the need to socialize, so I lift my hand and take a step toward them. Their interest or perhaps concern seems divided, however, as they stop a hundred feet away from me, back up, and stop again. After a few seconds of what appears to be an earnest conversation between them while not looking at me, they speed down the road.

I am left feeling rather rejected and not sure how to interpret their behavior. The only conclusion I reach is that my presence out in the middle of nowhere and on foot disturbed at least one of them.

Could it be some kind of karmic payback, I wonder—my mistrust of humanity to find and take my water bottles in exchange for their wariness of me?

I resign myself to eating lunch washed down with lukewarm water and being pegged as someone between an outcast loner and dangerous stranger. In the midst of my solitary pity party, however, five horses appear out of nowhere and after seeing me, head in my direction. While not a horse person—having only been on the back of one twice—I enjoy the opportunity to reach across the barbed wire fence and scratch their ears and rub their faces. Our conversation is one-sided, but I think we all get something out of the encounter. My new friends accompany me along the road for a hundred yards before they give up and head back in the direction of the reservoir.

My spirits lifted by the encounter, I continue south for a few miles, but when the road angles to the left I jump at the chance to instead veer in the other direction. It's time to leave behind the roads, both new and old, and everything else that serves as a reminder of both current and historic civilization.

During the last few miles of the day, I hope to immerse myself into a desert landscape that is reaching its late-May peak bloom. While I passed scattered wildflowers throughout the morning, the ten miles covered so far has boosted my chances to see them in greater concentrations. The increase in elevation gained from working up through the Salmon Falls drainage, and closer proximity to the uplifted ridge, has improved the conditions needed for the showy forbs to prosper. The most stunning species comes in the form of large swaths of golden lupine that give off a sweet aroma that almost seems intoxicating. Red and orange paintbrush, grouped together in small patches, complement the mass of lupine and a sprinkling of bluebells. The efflorescence appears even more intense near the base of the foothills, so I continue in that direction.

While walking I contemplate the shift in color observed while passing across southern Idaho since January. The dull browns and grays of last year's decadent vegetation that dominated the winter eventually gave way to a flush of green, but it took several more weeks before new life really took hold. Now most of the forbs and native bunchgrasses are nearly finished growing and have entered their bold stage of reproduction.

The proximity of the ridge permits me to enjoy the scene of stacked layers of basalt that comprise the high country. I savor the idea that the flows were once connected to those underneath my feet before becoming fractured and thrust 1,500 feet upwards over time. The combination of the geological past as a backdrop to the vegetative present paints a dramatic picture.

It is only when I swivel my head around to take in the whole scene that I notice a thunderhead cloud that has been growing about ten miles back to the south is now tossing an occasional bolt of lightning. As I walk in that direction and consider my lack of shelter if the storm edges closer, a few beams of angled afternoon sunlight pierce the overcast sky and light up a small area a half mile away. Much to my surprise and delight, five pronghorn antelope are illuminated by the spotlight. I look at the animals through binoculars, lower them to absorb the grand view, and then repeat the process several times. The show is soon over as the sun's rays disappear, but the scene is burned into my brain. The only downside to the moment is Beth's absence. After the tortuous walking she endured last month, she deserved to see that. The vision amidst the painted landscape moves me to make sure to invite her along for a short hike here next weekend.

As the thunderstorm moves safely away, the best of the wildflower displays continue to draw me toward the edge of the bench. Staying tucked up against the hillside also allows me to bypass private property that lies close to the upper end of the reservoir where several streams trickle into it. One of those is Browns Creek, again of that earliest settler fame, which I cross. A few miles later I intersect China Creek, named after those men who helped build the freight road. The creeks' flows will diminish as summer dominates and dries out the land, but for now a few remnant snowdrifts hanging along the top of the ridge help keep them gurgling.

After I loop around the private property and begin to head back down toward the upper end of the reservoir, I notice dust from a car driving the main road that lies not much more than a mile away. Looking through binoculars, I confirm that it is my mother's vehicle. In addition to the good timing, I even manage to call her on my phone, although the reception is sketchy out here. After giving her my location, I am told that she, her friend, and my sister will enjoy the scenery and eat lunch while they wait for me. The arrangement works out well for everyone.

Chapter 12

MAY 31

Beth readily accepts the chance to venture out the following weekend and see the wildflowers that dominate parts of Browns Bench. The side trip will not count as official progress toward reaching the Nevada high country by this fall, but that's part of the point. The day's decree calls for enjoying ourselves in the simplest manner possible. We decide to explore the area first while driving and then walk in whatever direction moves us. After having seen our fill, we can simply return to our pickup and go home. No specific end goal or logistics will exert control over us.

When I tell an acquaintance about our vague plan, he suggests we check out a tributary to China Creek. The area is called Player Canyon, which given our desire for a laid-back outing, sounds appropriate. The small gorge is another of those that channels a trickle of water out from the long ridge overlooking Browns Bench, but unlike the rest contains an old jeep trail through its entire course. The gain of a thousand feet in elevation is spread out over a couple of miles—the type of climb not experienced so far this year. And the outing still aligns with our desire to walk only as far as we want and then just turn around.

On the drive along the same gravel road that I walked portions of the previous Saturday, we stop to visit with the small herd of horses who befriended me. After I introduce them to Beth and she takes both group and individual photos, we continue on the main road before finding a two-track that heads up toward the foothills. The wildflowers seen along the route across the bench are now a bit past their peak bloom, but still impress us. Another bonus near the end of the drive is the sight and sound of a stream of water that bubbles noisily from a hillside before tumbling into Player Creek. The random presence of the underground stream, known locally as Roaring Springs, makes it a delight to behold.

We leave our vehicle at road's end and enter the canyon on a path that appears to be used only by an occasional all-terrain vehicle. Minutes after our saunter begins we spy a pair of mule deer that launch themselves from the strip of forest growing along the stream. After they climb to a safe position and stop across from us, we distinguish that the duo both sport a set of three-point antlers covered with velvet.

My focus eventually falls back down to the dense corridor of trees that provided cover for the deer. While for the last five months I have appreciated the junipers and willows that thrive along the banks of Salmon Falls Creek, it is nice to see more diversity. A mix of birch, alder, chokecherry, mountain mahogany, and other deciduous shrubs and trees form a dense thicket that hides the gurgling creek only a stone's throw below us. In sections where our path dips closer to the stream, we walk through passageways walled off by the mass of vegetation. Where one tunnel ends and we bask in the sunlight before entering another, our boots brush lupine and groundsel sporting purple and yellow blossoms. The display at our feet, however, is obliged to compete with the fortress of rhyolite towers and hoodoos glued to the steep slopes on each side of the creek. Above those formations cirrus clouds are brush stroked against the canvas of blue sky.

Amidst the sublime scenery we revel in our freedom. The concept of time ceases to exist as we wander, stop, and often backtrack for a few steps to again look at or photograph an interesting plant or insect or rock. Several bumblebees and a swallowtail butterfly working over a small patch of flowers capture our attention. A purple-flowered plant called silky phacelia keeps the pollinators, along with Beth and me, particularly enthralled. The forb's name comes from the fuzzy appearance of its vertical cluster of flowers tipped by long filaments. Its novelty not limited to appearance, phacelia has the ability to accumulate heavy metals from the soil at such high concentrations that the resulting toxicity repels grazing mammals.

Within a couple of miles the trail begins to level off after reaching an elevation of seven thousand feet. The snow that accumulates and lingers in the swale at the top of the canyon provides enough moisture to sustain several small groves of quaking aspens. Not only are their dancing leaves and white papery bark stirring, but a few trunks contain historic carvings. While sheepherders followed their flocks through these hills starting in the late 1800s, it was the Basque immigrants that began arriving after the turn of the century who most often left their mark. The oldest arborglyph that I discover reads "Sep 2 1927."

After emerging from the top of Player Canyon, Beth and I feel little desire to proceed farther. When we turn to look back in the direction just traveled, we are provided with a clear view of the canyon's east ridge. Its mid slope is populated by groups of mahogany but without a doubt the main attraction comes as a pair of massive rock fortresses standing on the hillside's crest. Without much discussion we leave our path and begin to circle cross-country back toward them.

We soon set our sights on the saddle between the two rhyolite formations, but before reaching that destination we succumb to the allure of more wildflowers. While the shallow soil is composed mostly of red gravel not capable of sustaining much vegetation, the number of forbs just beginning their bloom comes as a surprise. Besides the usual suspects, paintbrush and lupine, we begin to notice tiny plants with blossoms held close to the ground. The delicate brown and white bitterroot, a Native American staple, blends in so well that we have to watch our step.

Our focus on the ground in turn alerts us to the occasional presence of the short-statured hedgehog cactus. Sometimes called mountain cactus, these round plants are also just beginning to produce yellow flowers from the center of their spines. Nearly all the cacti, about the size of a flattened baseball, grow in isolation from each other. The exception is one group of much smaller plants clumped together. My count of thirteen makes me feel nothing but lucky since this find is only the second time that I have stumbled upon the species. The Simpson's hedgehog cactus, in fact, has only been found in four Idaho counties and is classified as rare or uncommon.

Once we climb to the top of the ridge and begin enjoying the elevated view, I check my map for the first time that day. I orient myself and notice that the rock formations a hundred yards to either side of us actually have names! The larger of the two, Steamboat, rises to our south, while Little Tug, in a slightly lower position, lies in the opposite direction. While we are too close and likely at the wrong angle to see if they resemble the watercraft they are named after, I make a mental note to look up here during next month's journey.

The views below us of Browns Bench and the reservoir, along with that of China Mountain and its creek and canyon, are pleasing, but they seem like more of an afterthought. The satisfaction comes from sitting and absorbing our more immediate surroundings that include the scattering of flowers and the massive stone formations painted with gray, yellow, and orange lichen. The tranquility is only interrupted when a shadow races across our feet. We look up to see that the disruption belongs to a golden eagle that flew from the direction of Steamboat and is now floating down toward Little Tug. The bird banks around the outcrop and is not seen again. Our trance broken, neither Beth nor I still speak of leaving.

Chapter 13

JUNE 11

A couple of weeks after the enjoyable outing at Player Canyon, I drive the Browns Bench gravel road one more time and stop near the upper end of the reservoir. The day's plan consists of following Salmon Falls Creek upstream to where it intersects Highway 93 a few miles south of Jackpot, Nevada. Before that hike can commence, however, I walk China Creek's final mile.

As the stream flattens out and slips through a meadow on its final approach to the reservoir, piles of rock attract my attention. Some of them run in straight lines and intersect at right angles, while one exhibits a graceful curve. I don't know how long ago they were constructed, but in 1894 Nora Sparks filed on this land that became a tiny piece of the Sparks-Harrell enterprise—one of the largest cattle operations in the region. After inspecting a rock wall that appears to have been a circular corral with an eighty-foot diameter, I peer in the direction that China Creek flows.

When southern Idaho and northern Nevada receive decent snowfall over the course of a year or two, the spring melt and ensuing runoff can back the reservoir up beyond the mouth of China Creek. After a pair of dry winters followed by this year's average snowpack, however, no evidence of captured water exists. A month of irrigation demand by this season's crops on the Salmon Tract has also pulled that much more from the impoundment.

Instead of terminating with a vivid entry into the backwaters of the reservoir, China Creek instead wanders out of sight into an expanse of weeds growing from the dry bed. I shadow the current for two hundred yards until it mixes with the murky flow of Salmon Falls Creek. While pleased to see my companion again, the overall scene underwhelms me. But then again, that's life in the West. Periodic drought serves as a reminder of how dependent we all are on water and how it is often taken for granted. The sight is also a reminder of the inflated promises made here, and on many other irrigation projects, that reached beyond the landscape's ability to deliver.

I plod upstream along the twisting creek as it cuts through unstable banks built with sediment that for a century was deposited from erosion occurring at higher elevations. With the absence of consistent water here at the upper end, annual weeds are guaranteed to flourish. The combination of new spring growth and the remains of last year's plants team up and attempt to trip me. On one occasion they succeed and I execute a slow-motion fall that delivers me into the skeletons of a cocklebur patch. After extricating myself from the mess, I remove my shirt and spend several minutes picking off the spiked seeds.

The vegetation thins out as I work southward, and after a mile of walking through the empty reservoir I reach its upper boundary. Willows and other perennial water-loving plants begin to line the creek that now flows through a canyon so shallow I'm not sure it can still carry that label. The greenery extends away from the water for about fifty feet on either side. After angling up to the low rim where I gain a better perspective, the scene just visited grabs me. That vibrant strip of vegetation that taps into the floodplain's moisture serves as a striking contrast against the brown rimrock, tanned curing grasses, and gray sagebrush that comprises everything else.

The view reminds me that while summer is ten days away on the calendar, its presence seems to have already been made known on the high desert beyond the corridor's haven. The wild colors of flowers that dominated Browns Bench several weeks ago have also vanished. The only blooms of note—red or yellow—sit atop an occasional prickly pear, a cactus-like species with a unique ability to store moisture. As my attention is pulled back to the oasis bordering the creek, it is only then that I become fully attuned to another sensory gift: an intense chorus delivered by songbirds gathered in the willow thickets.

After hiking in or along the edge of the shallow canyon for an hour, I make a slight detour and hike to the top of a small rise. The spot rewards me with just enough elevation to obtain the first unobstructed view to the west since I left my vehicle. After searching the uplift above the bench for the canyons cut by China Creek and other streams, I let my eyes wander. The profiles of two distinct rock outcrops on the skyline shock me: Steamboat and Little Tug! The resemblance is so uncanny that I cannot help but fixate on their silhouettes. The only improvement to the vision might include a few clouds drifting from right to left to give the illusion that the smaller boat is pulling the larger. Only when I begin to walk again, while turning my head to the right to keep them in sight, do I remember standing between the outcrops with Beth and telling myself to look westward from down here.

Gazing back down toward the creek, I spy a two-track that winds down into the drainage from the opposite side. I realize that the road leads to a canoe and kayak takeout for voyages that begin where the creek flows underneath the bridge on Highway 93—my destination for the day. The paddle downstream speaks of another of Salmon Falls Creek's unique features as one of only a handful of small streams for a hundred miles in any direction that has decent, floatable water.

I made the float trip fifteen years earlier with my teenaged son. Prior to our journey, several people who had made the voyage expressed some exasperation due to the creek's unceasingly twisty nature. Keegan and I confirmed that the creek, flowing that day at about five hundred cubic feet per second, required diligence in positioning the canoe correctly as we were thrust into each bend. While never reaching a state of frustration, we were not unhappy to pull the canoe from the water after the challenging half-day float.

As I eye the takeout and recall that April day, two other things stick out in my mind. One concerns a spot upstream in Nevada where a low concrete dam extends across the creek. The structure serves as a barrier to keep walleye, a voracious predator that had been transplanted into the reservoir, from swimming into the upper reaches of the drainage and feeding on native redband trout. While Keegan and I had no difficulty portaging around the dam, we did get hung up on a submerged boulder immediately after resuming our float. The rock turned out to be the only serious obstacle, aside from the willow thickets along the bank, that we needed to avoid during our entire trip. And we, of course, ended up right on top of it. My son and I eventually completed a 180-degree spin before finally inching off the rock backwards—all while trying to not panic. Reflecting on that near mishap brings forth the vision of Beth and me back in February performing our quarter-rotation on another boulder.

Along with those two memories, a third comes rushing in concerning an occasion long ago when my brother and I swamped the same canoe near Balanced Rock in December. I have never put the three memories together until now and can only come to one conclusion: perhaps I should not encourage my family, or anyone else for that matter, to accompany me in that canoe and on this creek.

The other thought settles on how different generations might approach the same adventure. While we held some common motives for making the trip, Keegan seemed focused on speed and pushing the canoe down the creek. During the last half of the trip I imagine he grew tired of the continual back-and-forth and became eager to get off the water. He paddled with increasing conviction as the day progressed. On the other hand, I was quite content to sit in the back, use my paddle as a rudder, and occasionally make a stroke for alignment purposes. I wanted to relax, enjoy the constantly evolving canyon, and prolong the time spent on the creek with my son. As he paddled harder, I found myself countering that additional forward momentum by twisting my blade into a braking position. I never confessed my offense to him, but I believe we both went home happy.

I descend from the small hill that provided the satisfying view and reflections and take up the familiar role that began in January—walking the rim. The hiking now, however, is beginning to have a different feel to it. This landscape is unknown to me except for that limited perspective from a canoe inside the canyon. I am the farthest from home yet on this venture and now about to cross into another state. And I am alone.

While I have brushed up against all those pieces this year, they haven't all come together until now. And it's the solitude that has the most profound effect. While spending ten days with my wife exploring this drainage gave me a set of experiences that I will treasure forever, another part of me still longs for occasional solitude. I do not compare the scenarios as one being better than the other. They each have their appeal depending on the place and my frame of mind. My desire and reward from connecting with a landscape that provides me spiritual nourishment cannot be easily disregarded. Sometimes I need to share the experience with people, but at other times am overcome with the need for a solo journey. A certain level of discomfort and anxiety has always pressed down on me when surrounded by too many people. That smothering sometimes can only be mediated by solitude. I feel the need to escape and lose everyone—including myself. While alone I rarely feel lonely and am often able reach a state where my thoughts settle down and even disappear—unless they have something to do with the country that accompanies me.

By late morning I have covered enough miles to slip into that quiet space. There is little for me to think about, and although my hip started hurting earlier, even that discomfort has been shed. For no particular reason, having evidently lost what might be considered a conscious plan, I drift away from the canyon rim. Moving through the low sagebrush I notice a single nighthawk swoop past me, then a few more a hundred yards out, and still more past them. I see at least a couple dozen birds over the course of the next half mile. More often a solitary type of bird, their gathering is by far the biggest concentration of nighthawks that I have ever witnessed. At some point their performance brings me to a halt, so I just stand and marvel.

The nighthawks dip and twist and rise again in a smoothly erratic flight; at certain angles I catch a flash of the white blaze beneath a wing. They seem to care little about my presence, especially after I sit down, and occasionally dart within thirty feet of me. I detect, even with my poor hearing, the soft nasal *peent* of their call. The most animated noise, one that I have never heard before, comes as a soft boom as they occasionally near the ground. The sound, much like that of the quick roar of a large truck as it passes by, seems peculiar coming from such a slender, graceful bird. After I start moving again and the feathered fauna vanish one by one, the mystery of the encounter sticks with me.

Only later after returning home will I read about nighthawks and begin to understand their behavior. That the bird is not a hawk I already knew, but my association with them had been limited to seeing them on the farm. They show up there in small numbers, usually at dusk, and patrol the length of a canal to feed on airborne insects. This time I had the good luck to stumble upon them in broad daylight during mating season when the males perform their aerial movements that are used, not surprisingly, to impress potential mates. And as witnessed, the unique display is not simply visual. The outburst at the bottom of that sweeping dive is created by the sudden force of air pushed through the male's primary feathers located on its wingtips.

With the nighthawks behind me, I notice a small gorge sneaking in from my right and heading toward Salmon Falls. It contains Cottonwood Creek, the most significant drainage coming from the high country above Browns Bench. Assuming that the overlook between the two canyons will be a good spot to relax, eat, and indulge in a good view, I change course and angle in that direction.

Only while checking the map during lunch do I realize that within the last half hour my feet and legs propelled me into Nevada. Earlier in the hiking project I assumed that reaching the border would be cause for a satisfying recognition of crossing from one state into another. Lost in the walking, however, I had not thought to look at the map for a while. I understand now that the last east–west fence I crossed served as a demarcation between states. Since there had been no "Welcome to Nevada!" sign placed out in the middle of nowhere for random hikers like me, my chance for anything celebratory had passed. On the other hand, my random route that took me through the land of nighthawks did occur close to the state boundary. Maybe I will just consider them as my welcoming committee.

As I sit and enjoy entry into the Silver State, more birds continue to entertain me. After watching a pair of red-tailed hawks make several tight circles on the other side of Cottonwood Canyon, a shadow passes near me. I look up toward the overhead sun and spot the profile of a turkey vulture riding the warming air currents. The intersection of shadow with human here on the ground is purely coincidental—the bird has no interest in me. A keen sense of smell drives its search for carrion, not the sight of an animal's presence, dead or alive. While I likely don't smell very good after hiking during the warmest weather yet encountered this year, things will have to go quite poorly for me before becoming attractive enough to the soaring bird.

Once lunch is finished I hike two hundred yards upstream along the rim overlooking the Cottonwood drainage before finding a place to drop down into its shallow canyon. After working across, up, and out of the basin, I continue my journey south along Salmon Falls Creek before intersecting a transmission power line that has jumped over to my side of the canyon. If that construction isn't a powerful reminder of civilization, with the thick wires hanging from the tall steel towers, I don't know what is. The hum emanating from the lines, which cannot only be heard but felt, keeps me from lingering. The presence of all that electricity then brings to mind the fact that the gambling town of Jackpot and its flashing, noisy slot machines are only two miles away. I pick up my pace as if putting more space between me and the highly charged local landscape will also mentally distance me from them.

I soon find out that it does not, but in a way that surprises me.

No longer intent on seeing every piece of canyon, I decide to shorten my remaining distance by angling from one bend to the next. Not long after beginning my first shortcut, I find a golf ball half-buried in the soil near a sagebrush plant. In any other place the find would baffle me, but I immediately know where it came from—back toward Jackpot.

My advisor for floating this stretch of creek, Rich Yankey, once told me that while volunteering for a wildlife agency he sometimes came across a golf ball whenever he got within a few miles of town. He reasoned that the balls came from a golf course on the edge of Jackpot. Asked how that might be possible, he contended that ravens, known as notorious egg predators, mistook the balls for a meal and flew off with them. Once away from the scene of the crime, the bird might purposely drop the ball to break it or land with the object to enjoy a feast. I could not help but wonder if such an intelligent bird might feel a little disappointed upon realizing there was no reward for its thievery.

After hearing Rich's theory, a little research seemed necessary to explore the possibility of that mischievous sequence of events. I was pleased to confirm that the phenomenon of ball-stealing ravens has been reported across the country and even in Scotland, where the sport of golf began. On at least one course golfers were advised, since it was assumed that white balls were more easily mistaken for eggs, to instead use something with color. While that approach sounded plausible, I find fault with the idea. Three miles away from the Jackpot course, the dimpled sphere that I hold is orange.

After finding another ball a few minutes later—this one white—I set my sights on a small rise about a mile away. On the other side of the hill lies the intersection of Salmon Falls Creek with the highway. And at the crossing's rest stop Beth will greet me and offer me cold water. The moment will not come soon enough—the temperature has risen into the mid-eighties for the first time while hiking this year, and what little water I have left is unappealingly warm. While the map offers a primitive road that bends around the south side of the hill and meets the highway about a mile from our planned meeting spot, my impatience moves me to take a more direct approach. I hope to find passage along the north side of the hill near the creek, and if that does not work out, maybe just go up, over, and down the modest bump on the horizon.

My loyalty to the creek does not pay off. An attempt to head up and around the hill ends as the slope steepens and then transitions into an impassable cliff. I backtrack a bit and then commit to a full descent, hoping for a ribbon of walkable ground next to the creek. A thicket of willows, a daunting pile of fallen rock, and the bottom of the cliff block that route. The other side of the creek looks equally difficult, leaving a wade upstream as the last option. That passage appears possible, at least for the first fifty feet, but the thought of wading upstream through murky water of unknown depth leaves me, a certified non-swimmer, feeling uneasy. I give up and retrace my steps back around the hill while considering my two remaining alternatives. Whether influenced by unease, stubbornness, or haste, I again forego the safe bet and charge straight up the slope.

At the summit it becomes obvious that I have chosen wrong for the second time in the last half hour and that I should quit calling this obstacle a hill. The top of the bluff in relation to the highway and rest stop is much higher than I realized, even though I have driven by here at least a dozen times. A quick check of my topo map confirms that the elevation difference is four hundred feet, which leaves me feeling like an idiot. The slope is also quite severe—as in way too steep to make a descent. There are, however, a couple of silver linings to my regrettable position. I have been rewarded with a novel view of Salmon Falls Creek meandering across an open plain. For the first time in seventy miles, the stream is not bound by even a hint of canyon.

The most satisfying part of the scene is that of my wife standing in the parking lot below me. Although she is barely over a hundred yards away, cell phone coverage is marginal and it takes several attempts to connect. We discuss strategy and Beth confirms that a safe way down in the vicinity of where I stand does not exist.

Out of water and starting to feel a little weak in the legs, the idea of another detour does not thrill me. I mentally kick myself again for my choices that have led me all over and then on top of this unforgiving bluff. Besides not being nearly so worn out right now, cold water could be slipping down my throat. With no other options, we both start walking back to the south, with Beth next to the highway and me on the bare ridge. She locates a couple of routes that appear promising to her but from my vantage point and mental state still look too steep. We are forced to hike nearly a half mile farther before I find a comfortable spot to scramble down.

Upon reaching flat ground and reuniting with Beth, she surprises me with that cold bottle of water that I have obsessed over for the last several hours. While I assumed that anything liquid had remained in the car, she had been carrying it all this time. As we walk back to the car, buffeted by semitrailers that blow by us in the heat, I ponder my good fortune to have married such a considerate woman.

Chapter 14

JULY 17–18

A month after the convoluted finish that led to several dead ends, my son drops me off a half mile up the highway from that obstructive bluff. Planning for the latest leg of my journey along Salmon Falls Creek has not been without challenges. For the first time this year I have no canyon rim to serve as a guide, and the next twenty upstream miles flow entirely through private property. In addition, Highway 93 often runs within a quarter mile of the stream along that stretch. During the last several months I have become accustomed to the quiet and comfort of big spaces. Hiking next to the stream and nearby traffic, even if public access was available, holds little appeal.

The solution to my dilemma comes in the form of a minor mountain range that runs parallel to the creek for most of the desired distance. The crest of the Granite Range is never more than five miles to the east, so those highlands become my focal route. In addition to its relative proximity to the stream, the range stands a couple thousand feet higher. Mid-July temperatures well into the nineties would become a force to reckon with while attempting to cross open ground along the valley floor. Hiking at an altitude near 7,500 feet should offer cooler air and perhaps some cover.

Having never visited the Granites, I do not know what else to expect from the mountains other than what I learn from a BLM employee and a cowboy who once rode that country. There are a few springs that consistently supply water, while others likely dry up with the arrival of summer. Pockets of green vegetation will be present in the highest country, but I expect the most plants to exhibit various hues of brown and yellow. Another seasonal indicator is that several fires are burning across southern Idaho and elsewhere at lower elevations and the entire region is starting to fill with haze and on some days, outright smoke.

Summer may not be the best time to explore the desert, but I remain committed to complete one trek per month. In addition, with each journey taking place farther from home, my strategy has evolved and required a major change: no more day hikes. I need to cover more miles per outing, utilize my time better, and require less of my family in delivering and/or retrieving me. And that push toward self-sufficiency means that it is time to start backpacking. While not ecstatic about carrying an extra burden in the heat, the chance to camp and observe new country during the day's best light—just as the sun rises and sets—appeals to me. The trade-off seems worthwhile.

Another detail that has come under more scrutiny over the last several weeks is that of my left hip. Still an original ball-and-socket version, albeit without much cartilage, the joint on occasion has become rather painful. Having been down this figurative trail nearly a decade ago with my other hip, I know how the journey eventually ends. With that in mind I have a brief discussion with my son before starting my hike from the highway. I ask him to check for phone messages during the morning in case walking becomes too unpleasant. With no guarantee of reception out here, we make plans for a worst-case scenario that entails me hitchhiking back to Jackpot.

The first few miles unfold with ease as I head into the cold dawn. The attention on my level of fitness soon disappears and shifts to the trip's first discovery. The road takes me to the former site of a Union Pacific railroad station named Delaplain. All that remain are a few large blocks of concrete that were part of the stop's buildings constructed in the mid-1920s. Nothing is left of the railway, officially abandoned in 1978, except for the bed that had been cut and filled to maintain a steady grade in each direction. A branch of the Oregon Short Line that was pieced together over several decades, the railroad eventually connected Twin Falls to Wells, Nevada, in hopes of providing Idaho with a direct market to California. The line not only transported livestock, copper ore from nearby Contact, and other goods, but also provided passenger service until 1965. Like so many other spur routes, it disappeared as the affection for the automobile blossomed and the business model of trucking freight was embraced.

Shortly after leaving the Delaplain site the road splits. The main fork heads toward Utah, now only thirty miles distant, and along the way traces part of the historic California Trail. I choose the less traveled route that leads me across the plain and toward what looks like a cluster of large hills. The three rises anchor the north end of the Granite Range, and the central one, Middle Stack Mountain, becomes my target.

After hiking on the dirt road for several miles, I encounter a local ranch hand as I cross a bridge that spans a waterless Trout Creek. Stopping his flatbed pickup truck, he questions me about being out in the middle of nowhere in July. From there the conversation turns to drinking water. Do I have enough? Do I know where to find some in the mountains? Upon hearing that I received some basic information from the BLM, he snorts and gets out of his vehicle. We spread my map out on the hood of his pickup truck and he locates a few springs, one just past Middle Stack, which should satisfy the afternoon's needs. After several minutes of conversing and pointing at the map, followed by some ranch talk, we part company. He likely doubts my sanity, if not my ability, but I appreciate his desire to help.

Within the hour I stop to talk to an older gentleman driving another flatbed truck. After some of the questioning is repeated, the discussion veers toward the subject of mountain lions. I learn that they roam all across the Granites and will occasionally kill an unsuspecting calf. He does not suggest that I might be their next clueless meal, but the possibility seems to be inferred. I wait for the question about whether I am packing a gun for self-defense, since people often wonder, but the conversation ends before we get there. After I offer my thanks for his counsel and assurance about keeping an eye out for what he refers to as "those big cats," he drives away.

Before the dust stirred up by his truck has a chance to settle, I bolt from the road and head cross-country up a slight incline toward the mountains. If I receive any more questioning looks and advice, I might be forced to call my son and tell him to come rescue me. I can hear the exchange in my head: "No, Keegan, my hip is fine but it seems I've lost my nerve to proceed. It's just too dangerous out here."

After a few hours of cross-country hiking, Middle Stack becomes less of a distant goal and more of an imminent landmark. The high country is becoming increasingly attractive, but its draw isn't just confined to looks. The forty-degree temperature enjoyed before sunrise is now only a memory and the air is steadily warming down here. Up there, it must be cooler. I am also beginning to experience the downslope product of the Granite Range: a gravelly soil created from its parent rock that has been eroding from the high country for eons. Its capability to absorb, retain, and transfer heat to the soles of my feet impresses me.

After working my way into the uplands, I stumble upon a livestock trough. My backpack, socks, and shoes are quickly shed. I then sit on the side of the metal container and immerse my lower legs into its liquid. The springwater is cold enough that after a few minutes I am forced to withdraw my numbed feet, let them thaw for a moment, and slip them in again. The process is repeated several times. The physical relief will only be temporary, but I try to lock in on the sensation so that perhaps conjuring it up later might bring some comfort. It seems that any means that might help me deal with the heat during this trip should not be dismissed.

By noon my feet have propelled me up to the shoulder of Middle Stack. During a typical day hike there would be little hesitation about a short detour to the top, but this trek has little allowance for side trips. I instead veer off to the east and intersect a decent dirt road that comes up from the Trout Creek drainage. I was told the route will worsen, but the map indicates that it should still lead me southward across the entire crest of the Granite Range. I glance back one last time across the plain toward Jackpot before my gaze shifts to the immense spread of scattered rock. While small, isolated outcrops dot the foreground of the ridge, larger concentrations of the gray stone rise eerily off in the distance.

The mountain range was created by granitic magma that pushed up through a layer of mostly limestone rock 150 million years ago. The product of this intrusion visibly dominates an area about fifteen miles long and ten miles wide, but has also affected the surrounding lowlands. I experienced an aspect of that earlier when walking across the soil that originated from the granite. Its porous, well-drained composition allows most precipitation to soak easily into the ground. In addition, the mountains do not rise high enough to collect and retain much snow through the winter. The result is that the range often fails to yield enough runoff in the spring for flows to reach Salmon Falls Creek directly or via Trout Creek.

Thinking about the landscape's dry nature reminds me of my own impending shortage. Before much hiking can be done along the ridge, I need to replenish my supply. The map shows one small blue dot that marks a nearby spring. I compare the symbol's location with the top of a quaking aspen grove protruding from a small draw about a half mile away. The map and scene appear to fit with this morning's discussion about a water source. Relief over the prospect of stashing full bottles into my backpack helps to quicken my pace.

The road meets and then runs next to the quarter-mile strip of aspens and shrubs that the BLM has fenced off from cattle. At the top end I drop my backpack, stuff four water bottles into a smaller knapsack, and walk over to the barbed wire fence to get a closer look. Seeing its four strands of tightly strung wire, I choose to remain on the outside of the fence and conduct an initial inspection from there. While nothing wet is discovered on the hike down, I flush a pair of deer from a cluster of aspens and walk underneath two juvenile red-tailed hawks sharing a nest near the top of a mature tree. After arriving at the bottom I carefully slip between a couple of the fence's unyielding wires, walk back up through the middle of the exclosure's trees and brush, and again come up dry. Any confidence once felt about my prospects for finding the spring leaves me.

After returning to the top end, I decide to retrieve something to eat from my backpack before continuing my search. As I crawl through the fence a second time, a wire barb rips a long slit through the thin fabric of my pants. Tracing the damage with my hand, I become dismayed at the amount of my backside and underwear that are now exposed. At least no one is around, and likely will not be for the rest of the trip, to get a good look. I drink the last of my warm water while considering the rare, but now obvious, need for my emergency sewing kit that I left at home. As I ponder not only the absence of a needle and thread but also my empty bottles, I look at the map and try to again guess the exact location of the spring. On my way back through the fence the menacing barbs receives a little more consideration.

While working my way back down the length of trees already walked twice, but this time on the other side, I discover a full trough across from the far fence line. I find that the pipe outlet is fully submerged and offers me no means to capture any clean, free-flowing water. There appears to be no choice but to fill from the container undoubtedly tainted by cow slobbers. Of course, I did stick my feet into a trough earlier, so perhaps it is only fair that I risk drinking some of their drool. As an extra precaution, iodine tablets are added to the four quarts of water that are first filtered.

I enter the exclosure one last time and locate the spring collection box that feeds the trough via an underground pipeline. Since the water source there is safe from bovine mouths, I consider the possibility of replacing what was just processed with this new discovery. I lift the cover off the top of the steel cylinder buried in the ground and take a look. Not only does an unappealing film mixed with decaying vegetation cover the water's surface, but the real kicker is the presence of a three-foot-long skin that has been shed by a snake. I close the lid and try not to think any more about where my water came from.

After putting on my backpack—one silver lining to the hunt for water was being unburdened for almost an hour—I follow the road up to the crest of the mountain range. As I head south the prevalence and variety of granite sculptures make the scene hard to fathom. I have seen nothing like it except for Idaho's City of Rocks fifty miles away. That I also have gained enough elevation to garner a better view down into the corridor that holds Salmon Falls Creek and the highway makes the experience feel even more surreal. With binoculars I confirm that the hustle of humanity continues but find that I do not care. That world below me seems much more removed than the few miles in distance and two thousand feet in elevation.

By six o'clock I have hiked more than a dozen miles and consider stopping. My original plan considered spreading the thirty-five-mile trek over three days. That approach would give me extra time to move unhurried and, if needed, find some shade if the afternoons became unbearable. This day still contains four hours of daylight, however, and the already tolerable higher elevation air has ceased to warm. It seems wasteful to not take advantage of the benign conditions and the satisfaction found from the rhythm of walking. In addition, the seemingly endless piles of spectacular granite keep pulling me forward.

But there is also another aspect to this ridgeline that has begun to push back at me. As fantastic as the landscape looks, it's starting to feel a little severe and unforgiving. I have seen very little wildlife; the only significant population of anything comes in the form of the stone statues scattered in all directions. The fact that this place is also so dry never leaves my mind. During the entire afternoon I found only one more water source, a trough filled by a pipe sticking out from a rocky hillside. Within a mile of my initial fill-up, the discovery added nothing to my supply.

The final omen has nothing to do with the earth I walk on, but rather the sky. The combination of still air and the limited visibility from increasing smoke has created a heavy, almost confining atmosphere. Without a good reason to prolong my stay, I begin to think about completing the trek in two days.

And so I walk and bear witness to the granite. Some rocks lie at rest as single boulders that range in size from bowling balls to automobiles. Most look to have been randomly sprinkled across the top of the ridge and down either side. In other spots the formations appear as if they are the tops of constructions that begin well below the surface of the ground. Some sport tight clusters of granite the size of large houses, while others consist of stacks of rock that tower well over a hundred feet in height. Regardless of size, most are crisscrossed with straight-line fractures running in several different directions. I push on into the summer evening and stop looking only when the silhouettes of the monuments begin to blend into the darkness.

The journey that began before sunrise ends after hiking over twenty miles. Besides the sense of achievement gained from a backpacking personal best, the effort means that the trek's remaining distance can be completed tomorrow. Little about the feat feels good to my body, but my bad hip and tender feet complain the most. After rolling out my sleeping bag and lying down, I am cheered to see that the haze directly overhead is thin enough to still see the shine of stars.

As I drift off to sleep, the rancher's warning about mountain lions slides into my head. The only means for protection would amount to a pocketknife or a few select stones from the Granite Range, but I'm too tired and relaxed to care. My only defense comes as a half-conscious dare sung inside my head: "Here, kitty, kitty…"

The warm night and predawn spent in a half-zipped sleeping bag seems hard to reconcile with how cold the previous morning was and that I am now at a much higher elevation. No doubt exists that this new day will be hotter than yesterday. My second concern is that I likely have not been drinking enough water and now possess only a quart. I still can't help but smile with appreciation, though, when I think about yesterday's cowboy and his concern about me finding enough water.

Where is my next refill? The map shows a couple of springs a mile ahead of me that appear to sit well below either side of the mountain range's crest. I contemplate the effort of having to scramble down and back up and that there is also no guarantee that the springs will be flowing. When the spot is reached and a decision necessary, I choose to remain on the ridge and keep walking. While the map offers several more prospects an hour away but near the road, nothing turns up there either.

No other option exists other than to keep walking south toward the tallest mountains in the range and where the largest concentration of springs dots the map. By the time I reach a meadow that looks promising, I have had nothing to drink for several hours. The clearing contains a very shallow pond on the far side, but I only find muddy water that a small herd of cattle were gathered in and fled from when they saw me. A portion of the pond is fenced off from livestock, but there is little standing water present amidst the moss and warm mud. I move on.

An hour later near the summit of Hanks Peak, I discover the first naturally flowing water since getting a glimpse of Salmon Falls Creek yesterday morning. The trickle is so shallow, however, that I have trouble getting water through the filter's intake hose without sucking in mud. I dig a hole using a stick and my hands to create a small pool, but find the results unsatisfactory. While my standards are lowering, desperation hasn't set in yet.

After snaking through a thicket of willows and aspens that line the tiny stream for about a hundred yards, I locate the flow's source oozing from between two large boulders. A short crawl between them brings me to a small clear pool about eighteen inches wide and six inches deep. The spectacle is no doubt the most heartening piece of nature that I have witnessed in a long time. Just before I start filtering, a chipmunk darts into the small cave from another direction. I cannot summon up much empathy for his needs and tell him as much: "Sorry, Hank—I was here first."

I spend a half hour in the shade of the boulders and trees while trying to filter and drink as much from the delicious spring as deemed reasonable. After filling my bottles, two of them are stashed deep in my pack in hopes that they retain, for as long as possible, the cool underground that birthed their liquid. The thought of drinking more warm water has become increasingly repugnant.

Loaded up and ready to continue, I step back out under the sun and continue on the two-track that led me up into this small drainage. The road contours around the north side of Hanks Peak and then bends back around the opposite slope of a nearby twin-summited mountain. The landscape undergoes a sudden transformation toward the end of the serpentine when the granitic stone that has accompanied me for so long vanishes. The White Peaks instead feature a gravelly limestone and look exactly as advertised. The road ends when I reach the saddle between those knobs and China Mountain. The range's highest summit at just over 8,300 feet in elevation, the peak is also the final one in the string of mountains as it makes a finishing twist toward Salmon Falls Creek.

Part of me again cannot help but advocate a walk to the summit. I reason that it would take less than an hour, but the suggestion is shouted down by the survival-mode contingent growing inside of me. Before continuing I sit down, remove my shoes, and eat lunch. The elevated terrain also provides me with excellent phone service, so I call Beth and tell her of my change in plans. We agree on a place where the highway crosses Salmon Falls Creek and a time that should give me ample opportunity to arrive first. Before resuming the journey I tend to a couple of hot spots that have begun to develop underneath the second toe on each foot. Not often prone to blisters and never there, I attribute it in part to the reliably hot soil that my feet have trod over the past two days.

Now at the end of both the mountain range and the road, my route consists of a plunge off the edge of the high country. I ease down the steep pitch while trying to keep my top-heavy profile from tipping me into a backside skid or forward fall. While the crest of the entire range has been nearly treeless, the north-facing slope that I slide down supports a scattering of quaking aspens and lush shrubbery. Grabbing onto a branch whenever possible helps me stay upright and serves as a braking aid. After a half hour of progress drops me fifteen hundred feet in elevation and exhausts my knees, the steepest piece of the descent ends at China Mountain Spring. While my backpack still holds plenty of water, I take advantage of being able to drink something cold again.

Before continuing, I spot two flocks of chukars that are each composed of a scattering of small chicks and a parent trying to keep their attention. It's hard not to be impressed and a little jealous of how quickly the tiny game birds scurry up the far hillside. As the two groups angle off in separate directions, I find a worn path that heads down a ravine. The trail soon becomes a four-wheel-drive road, and before I realize what has happened, my feet have returned me to flat ground. The sudden transition to the desert swelter makes the last spring and verdant mountainside seem like a fantasy.

Instead of heading directly to the highway, I angle a bit to the north. The route will cost me an extra mile, but I want to give Beth an easy landmark—the intersection of creek and highway—to retrieve me from. By mid-afternoon I reach the same power line that I walked underneath last month while near Jackpot. I remember being somewhat repelled at the time by all that electricity and what it represented, but today I couldn't care less. I pass underneath the hum and stop at a smaller line with wood poles running parallel to the first. This one has a maintenance road that runs underneath, so I follow its tracks.

Maintaining a good pace in the ninety-degree heat becomes a struggle. As my stride shortens into what seems like a plod, I begin to regret walking the extra distance. Setting goals soon begins to take on importance, so I walk to every other power pole before taking a break. Standing briefly in the shade of their fifteen-inch width does not compare well to taking refuge underneath a quaking aspen, but it is better than nothing. As my drive lessens I adjust my goal to just reaching the next pole. After completing a few of those seven-hundred-foot segments, I finally come within less than a half mile of my destination. I allow myself a quiet celebration and change course, but my victory march toward the creek ends suddenly when one of my blisters pops.

During my wife's several occasions of walking on compromised feet, I tried to be as sympathetic to her plight as possible. When the bubble underneath my toe gives way, however, I realize that I had little idea how it felt. Perhaps by going the extra mile today I got the opportunity to feel just a piece of her pain. That thought stays with me as I limp down the stream bank, yank my shoes and socks off, and stick my feet into the creek's welcoming water.

Chapter 15

AUGUST 31–SEPTEMBER 1

When I first considered exploring the Salmon Falls Creek drainage, the idea of hiking throughout most of the year sounded reasonable. Winter seemed to garner most of my attention since the planning for and the venture itself both began then. On the other end of the timeline, I needed to finish up with the mountains before much snow fell. Candid thoughts about crossing the desert during the warm middle months, however, were pushed to the back of my mind. Some of those trips might be uncomfortable. There was no way around that possibility.

While I normally head to the mountains in the summer like most people, part of me instead started to embrace the opportunity of navigating the lower elevations. I would have the chance to discover the essence of a landscape at a time of the year when it was typically avoided. Beth and I had faced adversity in the midst of that forceful March wind that barreled through the canyon, but came away with an experience that we won't forget. I wondered what a July hike in the desert might be like and assumed it too would be a challenge.

In retrospect perhaps I held an overly optimistic or even idyllic view of how a summer backpack in the heat might unfold. The vision of an effort and the actual event, of course, often do not match up. In my case the two-day jaunt in July that covered about thirty-five miles was one of the most difficult trips that I have undertaken. Were some strategical errors made along the way? Should the trip not have been shortened by a day? I am not sure. I wrestled with several scenarios in hindsight but then decided that the only criticism that really held water was obvious—I should have drunk more water. But at times even then I was dependent on an unpredictable supply.

That there might be consequences from the ordeal first became apparent when Beth called to confirm my location no more than five minutes after I stuck my feet in Salmon Falls Creek. After putting my socks and shoes back on and scrambling up the highway to locate her, a intense wave of nausea and light-headedness forced me to grab onto the guardrails of the bridge. While waiting for the feeling to pass, I spent a surreal moment thinking about how ironic it would be if there had been nothing there to prevent me from toppling back into my creek.

After regaining my balance, I saw my wife parked in a turnout about a hundred yards away. Upon hobbling down to meet her, I found that she was again thoughtful enough to bring along an orange and a cold sports drink. After slowly consuming the fruit—it had to be the best one ever tasted—and finally sipping something not tinged by the flavor of iodine, I lay back in the seat while she drove me home.

After a few days I regained the five pounds that my body lost during its encounter with heat exhaustion. Most of me soon felt little worse for wear—except for my hip. The pain had become sharp enough that family and coworkers started quizzing me about my new limp. Only to myself did I first admit that perhaps the hiking had been overdone. A pair of visits with different doctors confirmed that the joint had been without most of its cartilage for quite some time and the ball at the head of the femur was deforming from wear. The diagnosis was no surprise, however, since at the time my other hip was replaced nine years earlier, the doctor said the one now in question did not look much better. While disappointed about the deterioration and pain, I did find some satisfaction as to having gotten quite a bit more mileage out of it.

The surgeon said that he could fit me into his schedule for some replacement parts, but I informed him that anything that drastic would need to wait. I figured about eighty thousand more steps were needed from the hip to propel my body across the remaining high desert and mountain terrain. To get through the next few months, we opted for a regimen of anti-inflammatories and an as-needed dosage of prescription painkillers. When the latter seemed to have little effect, and not willing to assume the risk of increasing the amount, I ended their use altogether. A cortisone shot during the second week of August helped to lessen the pain. After then hearing about a pulse of cool air that would arrive on the final day of the month, I decided the time had come to resume hiking.

After driving my pickup to the outing's endpoint and leaving it there, I ride back with my mother, her friend, and my sister to the spot where Beth found me six weeks earlier. As I slip on the backpack, my mother eyes the barren landscape and asks me if I really needed to be doing this. What else could be offered but a son's typical response? “It's okay, Mom. I'll be fine.”

While now on the west side of the highway and angling away from the Granite Range, I still find myself on the border of that magma intrusion that delivered so much gray and pink rock to the earth's surface. The picturesque formations witnessed during my last trip, however, are absent. Instead the granite appears most often in the form of unattached boulders scattered along the bottom of the Salmon Falls Creek drainage and up the nearby hillside.

The local mineral of focus came not from what composed the boulders but as a by-product of the chafing of the granite on other rocks as it pushed upward. Copper became king here and drew prospectors as long ago as the 1870s. With a nod to that long-ago interaction, both a mining district and eventually a town were given the name of Contact. The onset of the metal's removal and processing coincided with the establishment of the Toana Road and provided freighters with a destination to back haul needed supplies from Boise City. Prior to the town's formal creation, a small hotel was built only a few miles from my drop point and doubled as a rest station for the Fast Freight Line.

I look at my map and locate clusters of white-shaded areas depicting private property holdings that intermingle with the yellow-colored BLM ground. As I plot a course into the midst of the checkered landscape, I remember looking at a current aerial photograph that shows scars from either hand-dug exploratory pits or activity around more-formal mine sites.

The 1872 Mining Law became another tool utilized by the government to promote settlement of lands that lay west of civilization. The legislation provided fortune-seekers with the right to explore the public domain for minerals and, upon discovery of something desirable, stake a claim. Obtaining a patent on the claim cost from $2.50 to $5.00 per acre, with the higher rate assessed for a lode or vein. This fee not only purchased the underground mineral deposits, but prior to 1955 gave exclusive rights to the claimant for the land surface containing them. In most cases the federal government required annual assessment work to be done to keep the claim valid.

Interested in exploring an area that contains a concentration of mining activity, I leave Salmon Falls Creek and angle uphill. Within an hour I discover a large shaft that had been excavated vertically into the ground. A twenty-foot-square grate sporting angle-iron bars with five-inch gaps between them spans the entrance to prevent humans and large animals from falling into the abyss. I try to walk out on a pair of the bars that run across the side of the opening but cannot advance more than a few feet. While there's no way to fall through, I find the encounter disturbing. It's not even comfortable spending a few minutes lying perpendicular to the bars, again on the edge of the grate, to see if I can see the bottom of the tunnel. Only after I turn away from the hole and begin scrambling down the hillside does the gnawing in my gut leave me.

Evidence of other past activity found on the lower slopes of Ellen D Mountain proves much less dramatic. I discover a scattering of small pits dug in search of minerals that once offered hope and if not prosperity, at least some sort of payoff. Claim markers in the form of wooden stakes and plastic pipe jammed into the ground also serve as signs of more recent optimism. On occasion I stoop down to grasp green-colored rocks that reveal the presence of oxidized copper. Each find makes me feel like I have made an important discovery and prompts me to consider the nature of mining in the West during more distant times. What would it have been like to work so hard for often so little, and when prospects diminished, be drawn to the latest news of discovery? And wonder again if that next spot might be life-changing?

As I contour clockwise around the base of the mountain, my vantage point gives me a clear view of a complex of meadows that lie to the south. Created by the purposeful diversion of Salmon Falls Creek, the green pastures make for a dramatic change from the tilted and poorly vegetated country that I pass through. The origin of the irrigated land and ranch infrastructure, called Vineyard, goes back to the mid-1800s and has served as the key component for several livestock enterprises. The spread, as well as other Nevada livestock outfits, has water rights that predate those on the Salmon Tract. The meadows are crucial for growing grass that is often first harvested for hay that can be fed later in the winter months and then grazed during the summer or fall.

The ranch and surrounding high desert were also a frequent setting for a black cowboy named Henry Harris. The occurrence of a non-white cowhand during the thirty-year period following the Civil War was not rare. Researchers estimate that of the country's 35,000 cowboys who then rode the range, at least 15 percent were black. Harris distinguished himself less for his skin color, however, than as a man who could work equally well with both horses and humans. Brought to Nevada as a houseboy by John Sparks, who at the time partnered in a large cattle operation and then later became governor of Nevada, Harris quickly developed into a talented rider and roper. He was later offered and accepted supervisory roles like wagon boss and ranch foreman.

Described as even-tempered, fair, and the type of man most cowboys wanted to work for, Harris held the distinction of running one of the few all-black outfits in the country. The demand for cowboys decreased, however, as open range shrank and the cattle trail industry ended, herds were devastated by the winter of 1889–90, and railroads spread across the West. Harris wanted to do nothing else and so continued to work for several of the region's largest remaining outfits that included the Sparks-Harrell, Vineyard Land and Stock, and Utah Construction companies. The diminishing presence of black cowboys did not keep him from being sought after as a boss—most white cowboys were equally satisfied to ride for him.

Harris continued to pursue his calling as a cowboy. Photographs place him at numerous spots in Nevada and Idaho, including one that shows him on a Browns Bench homestead that he filed on in 1894. Seven decades after his death in 1937, he was inducted into both the National Cowboys of Color Hall of Fame and the Buckaroo Hall of Fame.

A booklet by Les Sweeney documented a 2012 memorial ceremony for Henry Harris and a dedication for his sister and nephew. The following tribute was provided by Gene Hopwood at the event: "I'm sure that Henry had faced prejudice and discrimination, even persecution in his life because he was a Black man in his day, but he didn't let that define him or hold him back. Early in this life he found what he liked to do and became very good at it. He developed an extraordinary talent and ability as a horse man, stockman, and leader of men. So much so that 75 years after his death we are still remembering."

As my trek continues around the mountain, thoughts of the cowboy accompany me until I stumble upon another mine shaft. This one burrows horizontally into the hillside with the opening again blocked by iron bars. A sign declares the mine as unsafe and that "Stay Out—Stay Alive" is the recommended course of action if somehow the gate is compromised and access enabled. To drive the point home, the sign says that some the dangers associated with abandoned mines include "loose rock, bad air, cave ins, rattlesnakes, old explosives, rotten timbers, [and] falling." Having been underground in a lava tube once that required crawling on hands and knees, I wonder if the sign makers considered adding claustrophobia and the potential of total darkness to the list. Those alone would probably keep me from going underground again, but I concede that the warning as it now reads ought to be effective for most everyone. After taking a couple of photos, I am again content to leave a hole in the ground behind me.

Within an hour the landscape marked by its mining and ranching history is replaced by another that hints at something more. The granite speckled with gray, white, and pink grains has vanished and been replaced with the brown tones of rhyolite—the result of volcanic flows from a different time and source. While the sun that I walk into hinders me from getting a good look at today's destination, I can make out a gap in the jumbled canyon landscape that Salmon Falls Creek exits.

At dusk I roll out my sleeping bag within a few feet of the creek that eases out from between a maze of towering pillars. While having never visited this spot before, the rocks and stream appear much like they do near home at Balanced Rock Park. As I bask in the pleasant dichotomy of a familiar newness, a tingle of anticipation adds to the mix. I have reached the Bad Lands.

The insinuation of a place name certainly depends on the eye of the beholder. Some might think of this area as desolate country with nothing practical to offer like minerals or grass. Others might conjure up images of a landscape not only lacking value, but as a place to stay away from unless you were a desperado. For me the name suggests something more mysterious and thus incites a desire to explore. It holds the possibility of a place visitors can enter into and, at least for a while, lose themselves. The Bureau of Land Management classified this landscape as a wilderness study area, so they certainly thought that it held promise. With that label and the evocative name considered together, I don't foresee a downside. At the very least I will have the opportunity to bear witness to and meander through a half-dozen miles of untamed country.

The next morning I head uphill since it appears that walking near the creek will be impossible due to the barricade of cliffs that guard the water. The faint two-track that I continue to follow from yesterday allows me to gain five hundred feet of elevation over the next half hour. The route then bends sharply to the left and cuts northwest through the upper elevations of the labyrinth's stone creations. My map shows that the primitive road runs parallel to the creek from often less than a mile away and traverses the entire length of the Bad Lands. The path soon dissolves into nothing, however, when confronted with a gulch that angles steeply back down toward the creek.

The opportunity to hike cross-country energizes me. Whether formally designated or not, wilderness should be nearly untracked and with as few hints of human presence as possible. Part of the adventure often lies in finding one's own way. While I can still see a radio tower near the summit of Ellen D and a distant four-wheel-drive road on the other side of the main canyon, my immediate environment looks unblemished and inviting.

Once I slip deeper into the Bad Lands, the place begins to reveal some of its secrets. The rhyolite formations come in an infinite assortment of shapes and sizes. The hoodoos and towers and concentrations of rocks are not confined to the immediate vicinity of the creek, but spread back up along the steep hillside for an impressive distance. Often long linear outcrops, running in random directions, connect to another in a manner that blocks passage and causes me to backtrack and search for another route. I discover several natural arches—two that I take the opportunity to walk or crawl through. Near one I place my camera on a nearby rock, set the timer, and run to the opening. I make several attempts at my version of a selfie before my silhouette is deemed passable. A small voice in my head questions such behavior, but it's hard not to embrace the fact that this trip feels so much more enjoyable than the last one.

On two occasions I scramble down ridges that sweep toward the creek as it twists through the canyon, but each time am left standing at the top of a hundred-foot cliff that drops to the water. The proximity of the creek prompts thoughts of finding a passageway down, but the jumble of stone appears like it might swallow me up. Even if the maze did permit me access, I would likely have no way to move upstream from there. Success in reaching the creek would still be rewarded with an immediate return up the steep slope in order to resume westward progress.

When comparing the Bad Lands to the deep canyon wilderness study area in the heart of Twin Falls County, it takes little deliberation to conclude which place offers a more satisfying experience. In Idaho I felt that the presence of an occasional two-track road linked us to people who might be just around the corner and, by extension, to civilization that was never far away. The flat ground we trod and the possibility of phone reception made me feel relatively secure. The creek flowing through the deep canyon had been tamed by a dam that diverted nearly all of its water elsewhere. As much as I still love that stretch of canyon, it's understandable why, during the Idaho BLM's final evaluation, the narrow corridor of canyon had not been recommended for a wilderness designation.

In the Bad Lands, none of those influences dilutes its wildness. My journey through the rough-and-tumble landscape evolves into the most stirring outing this year. The solitude reinforces a bond to the land that moves me beyond easy description, and the absence of a path and schedule gives the trek a sense of simplicity. I just wander and let the landscape nourish my spirit. The experience is also intimate; rather than gazing at something from a distance, I am surrounded by the allure. That the Nevada BLM recommended the area receive full protection is not hard to understand.

After hiking a half-dozen miles through the Bad Lands, the rhyolite formations become scarce and the drainage opens up. I begin shifting, despite my resistance, back into an awareness of the rest of the world. Spread before me lies a large basin that supports numerous ranches linked together by a network of gravel roads. In several directions I see the specks of far-off cattle scattered across the gently rolling terrain. With the help of binoculars I spy multiple drainages that flow from the Jarbidge Mountains and head in my direction as they combine to form Salmon Falls Creek. And when I catch a glimpse of a couple ten-thousand-foot peaks across the basin, I am reminded that my ultimate destination is getting closer.

But before getting a start on the next trek that will put me at the foot of those mountains, I need to finish the journey at hand. My first task is to traverse several miles of low hills beyond the Bad Lands. The line chosen to reach my vehicle pulls me away from the main creek and toward a point where I can cross the drainage's North Fork just upstream from the meeting place with its southern counterpart. Before reaching the tributary, I jump a doe deer from a thicket of willows growing along the floodplain. Soon after that I come within fifty feet of a great blue heron stationed on the bank of the creek. I am not sure who is more surprised as the long-legged bird emits a single loud squawk and then flaps away in silence.

After removing my shoes, socks, and pants, I tie them into a bundle that is tossed across the ten-foot-wide stream. Far more time is spent to partially disrobe and dress again than cross the creek while carrying my backpack, but I don't give the delay much consideration. The two-day trek has been one completely absent of haste or concern. The wade comes to a short halt once I'm thigh-deep in this same water that has gripped my focus for the last eight months. I linger in the cool liquid for a moment and simply stare at the current as it slips around me. After I reach the far side and get organized one last time, the final mile uphill passes quickly.

Chapter 16

OCTOBER 4–5

During the Idaho portion of the hiking and much of it in Nevada, little thought was given to my final approach to the Jarbidge Mountains. For nearly all the outings, I could study topo maps and count on never straying far from the single blue line that depicted Salmon Falls Creek or the tight brown contours of the canyon on either side. Even when the Granite Range pulled me off course a few miles, the stream corridor was rarely out of sight or far from my mind.

On those occasions when the project's final thirty miles of hiking did receive some consideration, I never did come up with a definitive plan. My finger rarely made it upstream from where the creek's two main forks unite before funneling through the Bad Lands. While determining my path had been simple with just a single stream to focus on, the half-dozen named creeks that drain O'Neil Basin made it difficult to know which tributary, if any, might take possession of me.

During the week prior to that pivotal trek, I dedicated several hours to again staring at maps and comparing elevations, topography, and the presence of trails. The specific route across the basin became less of a concern as my interest shifted west to where the four most significant creeks exit the Jarbidge Mountains. I traced each watercourse upstream and studied its place of origin and relationship to the range's highest peaks. After a handful of the eight ten-thousand-foot summits survived my initial cut, I finally reached a decision.

Gods Pocket Peak appeared to be the highest point that the Salmon Falls drainage touched and was also one of three mountains in the range I had not yet climbed. How could I go wrong heading in that direction? Rather than using a tributary to guide me across the basin, I could instead aim for a cleft in the foothills where Camp Creek departs and walk straight toward it. After completing that transect, the final hike of the year would then begin by following a trail that shadows the stream. Within a few miles a fork in the path would climb out of the drainage, deliver me into its neighbor, and then circle toward my destination. Relieved about finally possessing a plan, I devoted no more time to scrutinizing maps or inserting variables into the route equation.

Shortly after the actual hike across O'Neil Basin begins and I find myself standing on a plateau near the confluence of the North and South Forks, my grand plan quickly crumbles. The panorama of the basin and the Jarbidge country is fantastic, but the search for Gods Pocket yields nothing definitive. Most of the high-country terrain from this angle looks about the same and fails to move me. What does gain my focus, though, is the spectacle of Marys River Peak. What about that mountain with the broad summit that anchors the south end of the range? The one standing off from the rest of the group and covered with the season's first dusting of snow? Even with an elevation measuring three hundred feet higher than Gods Pocket, I had dismissed her earlier due to the fact that the top of the Salmon Falls watershed did not reach her summit and was lower than Gods Pocket. Letting go of the idea that an ascent to the absolute top of the drainage was essential, the original computations and conclusions are jettisoned. I realize that my gut has overruled my mind.

The epiphany does not alter my plans for the current hike across the basin. I can still head toward the mouth of the Camp Creek canyon and then later in the month walk upstream on its trail. Instead of then leaving the main path, I would just follow the creek to its highest point and then make a final scramble to the summit of Marys River.

Even though the peak rises only about twenty miles from my starting point, I still won't try to reach it this weekend. While the journey across the basin will deliver me to the Jarbidge range in a relatively straight line, the meandering ascent through the last half-dozen miles of high country will occur at a much slower pace. That hike into the mountains also requires, for the first time this year, a return trip. In addition, I want to keep limiting my daily walking distance. Easing through the Bad Lands not only benefited me physically but made the trip more enjoyable.

The logistics to placing my pickup on the far side of the basin is also a factor. With each destination now a considerable distance from Castleford, getting my vehicle situated this time took over three hours. That piece of the trip included a few stops for my support group of Mom, her friend Leon, and my sister Leah to enjoy the scenery, take a few photographs, and allow them to get a feel for my impending hike. We then consumed another hour to drive back across the basin and deliver me to my starting point. By the time we part company and I start hiking, it is one o'clock in the afternoon.

The hike across O'Neil Basin will take me through a prime sage-steppe environment filled with native vegetation and wildlife like pronghorn antelope, sage-grouse, and smaller sparrow-sized birds dependent on the arid West's key shrub. At six thousand feet above sea level, the area receives more precipitation than most of Nevada—the driest state in the nation—and thus can grow a dependable supply of vegetation for both wildlife and cattle. The multiple streams that spill from the high country and thread through the basin make it even more inviting to those involved in the livestock business. With rights senior to those downstream in Idaho, the water is freely diverted to irrigate meadows that grow even more grass. The perennial nature of many of these creeks also means that drinking water for cattle is available year-round.

The prospect of those ranching opportunities drew the first white settlers to the basin. In the 1880s the O'Neil family moved into the area not to just run cows, but for the isolation. Often on the wrong side of the law, the setting offered sanctuary for them to live on the edge of society. The California natives only came here after being forced from their first Nevada ranching endeavor in White Pine County 150 miles to the south, where the family's patriarch and four sons earned considerable notoriety as bullies and cattle thieves.

While detained on charges of shooting a local rancher, the father was killed and two sons wounded when some of the area's more reputable residents stormed the jail. Even though one son was quickly acquitted and the other released, the O'Neils knew that they had worn out their welcome. The brothers moved their families to the head of what was known locally as the Little Salmon River. Although the landscape was new, the attitude of the O'Neils remained unchanged. With the concept of the West's arid grazing land based on open range, the remote area became a strategic fit for the clan to call their own.

Family members along with hired guns and thugs intimidated anyone who wandered into or even near the basin. Accusations of rustling and beatings were repeated in Elko County, and on more than one occasion the brothers and at least one sister were involved in shootings. Even though their bad behavior and brushes with the law persisted, the family was not held accountable through the court system. The basin seemed to represent the Wild West at its worst.

Over the years the ranching enterprise expanded and the O'Neils even branched out into running sheep, an animal they once diligently attempted to keep out of their territory. Financial success seemed to smooth out the ornery edges of two of the brothers, William and James, who in time garnered a better reputation. Their past misdeeds apparently forgotten or at least no longer held against them, the brothers became known and sought out as honest businessmen. James even gained enough respect in the community that he became a member of the Elko County Grand Jury.

The good times, however, were not sustainable. A severe drop in cattle and sheep prices in the early 1920s spelled the beginning of the empire's demise. The business, largely built on credit, soon fell apart. After the local sheriff sold off the ranch's remaining land and assets, the last of the O'Neil family returned to California with little of consequence other than leaving their name on a piece of landscape.

The first mile of my hike follows the rim of a shallow canyon that provides a good perspective down into the South Fork corridor. The creek, tucked away between a long narrow meadow and a boulder-strewn hillside, remains enveloped by a thick strip of willows. Tire tracks from a swather and baler are still evident in the meadow's short grass, now turned brown, from a summer haying operation. Around the next corner, but before I drop down from the bluff, my view upstream includes the sparkling water of the creek as it twists through a tighter gorge. Beyond that constriction the rimrock vanishes and the drainage widens into several large meadows. One pasture is sprinkled with tiny dots that through my binoculars I confirm as cows with calves soon to be weaned.

Once off the knoll I leave the South Fork and head west toward Marys River Peak. My trajectory soon intersects the basin's main north–south road that we drove on a couple of hours earlier. Not wanting to be bothered by anyone wishing to stop and chat, especially since the hiking has barely started, I stride quickly across the gravel. My line soon takes me across Canyon Creek and another meadow filled with cattle. The animals seem more curious than concerned, except for a pair of bulls who lift their heads and take a few steps in my direction. While they don't worry me, I have been around enough livestock over the years to know not to completely trust them. After removing myself from their space, I begin a gradual ascent that allows me to cross paths with animals that I can enjoy a bit more—a small flock of sage-grouse and a pair of antelope. Those iconic animals prompt me to remain attentive to the rich high-desert country that surrounds me.

By early evening I have only covered seven or eight miles and part of me questions my lack of progress. I remind myself, however, of the hike's late start, the October sun that seems to set too early, and my choice to slow down. Without a set destination at day's end, I keep heading toward the gap at the base of the mountains.

The route brings me close to the headquarters of a ranch on Cottonwood Creek—the second stream visited this year bearing that name—so I make a short detour and follow a gravel road down to a concentration of buildings spread out near the stream. The working ranch's evolution has garnered attention over the last several decades. In the 1990s when public grazing began to be viewed with an increasingly critical eye, the BLM began talking about fencing off creeks that were in poor condition and reducing the number of cows. The ranch responded by inviting a diverse group of people from both government and the private sector to help develop a new grazing approach.

The collaborative plan resulted in a strategy that split the ranch into thirty pastures. Cattle were rotated through each unit on a schedule that kept them from staying in any one place for too long. To help ensure the success of the high density/short duration grazing system, riders were utilized to keep cattle moving within and between pastures. As part of the holistic and intensive management, an animal often viewed as controversial by the ranching community was given more value. The ranch quit fighting the beaver and let the animal do its thing. In addition to the creation of wetlands valuable to both wildlife and livestock, the reservoir of underground water helped creeks flow later into the summer.

The Cottonwood Ranch is also unique in that it also provides outfitting guides for big-game hunts and other opportunities for visitors wanting to experience the West. I have heard that it might also serve evening meals to the public on weekends. Since it is Saturday night, I consider checking to see about that possibility. If nothing else, it would be satisfying to replenish my drinking supply with something out of a well rather than having to filter water from the creek.

I wander through the willows and cottonwoods in the failing light before finding a large log building that likely contains lodging and a dining area for its guests. Part of me fantasizes about walking in, introducing myself, and inquiring about a meal. The introverted side, the one comfortable wandering around solo and who at times shies away from roads and people, decides against such a bold move. All I can manage is to find a side door that accesses the kitchen. I stick my head inside and ask a surprised cook about filling my water bottles from an outside hydrant. She smiles and says, "Sure, that's fine," and goes about her business of draining a steaming pot of broccoli. I thank her and make a quick exit, but the sight and aroma and thought of cooked food, and maybe even sharing it with actual people, stays with me.

After my water supply is replenished, I retreat back up the hill and escape on a two-track into the sunset. I consider my attempt at social interaction and feel the ache of failure. For the first time this year, loneliness presses into me and I question parts of my solitary nature.

As a younger man I embraced the isolation while working our family farm positioned on the edge of the desert. The lifestyle and our physical placement at the end of a graveled county road helped limit interactions with other people. With a lifelong anxiety that could infect me when encountering people, especially strangers or those in groups, the rural setting was not only what I wanted, but what I needed. Or so I thought.

As I approached forty years of age, however, something began stirring inside of me. I sought more connection. Family gatherings seemed more pleasurable, and talking to neighbors or acquaintances felt desirable. Quitting the farm for health and economic reasons, as unsettling as the transition was at times, provided many benefits. A move into the role of public servant pulled me out of my comfort zone and helped me realize that too much isolation, either in the physical sphere that I had preferred or inside my head, was not healthy.

But the old habits and fearful thinking didn't just disappear. Their hold persisted and the anxiety created, ten years after that career change, can still sometimes grip, paralyze, or edge me away from where I would like to be. And in that darker place it's not hard to focus on my shortcomings and speculate on the experiences that I miss. And that also sticks with me as I walk into the fading light.

As the distance from the ranch grows, the gloom created by the frustrating visit slips away and dissolves into the dark. As is often the case with a little walking, the movement may not be able to solve any of life's challenges, but can at least give them some perspective. By the time I have covered a couple of miles, the last one needing a headlamp to light the way, my focus has shifted toward simply finding somewhere to sleep. I return to Cottonwood Creek, now flowing through public land, and pitch my tent in the middle of a meadow. While unable to fall asleep quickly, the periodic sound of distant cattle bawling due to the weaning of calves, along with the eruption and trailing off of yapping coyotes, keeps me company.

Once it seems like I have slipped into a restful sleep, the sound of a vehicle wakes me. The sun will not rise for almost an hour, but the realization hits me that since it is Sunday morning in early October, a good chance exists that someone is about to start hunting for something. I have no doubt, in this moment, about the pros and cons of separation from my fellow humans. Not wanting my small brown tent or me to be mistaken for a target during the unfolding dawn, I locate my headlamp and bolt from the tent. A short, futile attempt is made to scrape frost from the rain fly and a few more hurried moments spent to fold up my housing.

After my tent and other gear are gathered up and stuffed into the backpack, a brisk march delivers me across the meadow and in the opposite direction from the disturbance. A quick ascent up a slight rise beyond Cottonwood Creek and in my needed direction puts roads and the potential of hunters behind me.

As dawn breaks I discover that my position is now too close to the Jarbidge foothills to view Marys River Peak behind them, but I can clearly see the folds in the rising landscape where Camp Creek exits. With only seven or eight miles remaining, the morning hike proceeds at a more tranquil pace than its frenzied start. My companions for the day materialize in the form of antelope, with at least a single animal, but more often a herd, in view for most of the morning. One group in particular seems content to rush ahead of me, stop for a bit while I catch up, and then again bolt in the same direction. While the season for hunting them is likely open, they do not seem to take me as a threat.

By noon I reach my truck and consider driving promptly home. Excited to have finally arrived at the foot of the mountain range, but also drawn toward Camp Creek's ribbon of trees beginning to turn from green to gold, I cannot resist walking a bit farther. Freed of my backpack I hike down a rocky four-wheel-drive road that leads into the canyon. After wandering on the trail for a mile along the creek and through the radiant woods, I witness enough to know that Beth would enjoy seeing this too. And by next weekend the turning foliage should be near its peak.

Chapter 17

OCTOBER 11

After hearing about the Camp Creek drainage, Beth is eager to witness its autumn colors. Wanting to experience the scene for the first time in person, she holds off from looking at any photos from my brief excursion. Her ability to exercise willpower, I soon find out, pays off. When we ease our pickup down the canyon's rocky road the following Saturday and get our first shared glimpse at the bright foliage, it's obvious we will receive a spectacular show. The weather also seems cooperative by providing a deep blue sky and a few wispy clouds painted by random brushstrokes. And fortunately for me, next weekend's forecast hints of more of the same for the trek to Marys River Peak.

Once down in the canyon, our two-track road levels off and meanders through small groves of quaking aspen. The ruts that we follow upstream occasionally carry trickles of water running toward us. While walking the road last weekend, I discovered that the source came from the flooding of Camp Creek due to the construction of beaver dams. The wetness presents a small challenge to driving, but I can't find fault with an animal following its instinct.

At the dry trailhead we find a collection of four-wheel-drive vehicles and stock trailers, a corral with several tethered horses, and a large tent. The spot serves as a base camp for the Cottonwood Ranch outfitters where they can stockpile horses and supplies, organize their guests, and then pack food, gear, and hunters into the mountains. The sight reminds me that Beth and I likely will be the only humans in the drainage not involved in chasing deer or elk. Our desires, however, do have some similarity to theirs. We are hunters of a different sort, armed with cameras in search of scenery and an experience that will tie us to the land.

My wife and I stroll along the path while being dazzled by the full glory of the cottonwood and aspen. Their golden leaves, mixed with the greens and reds of alder, rose, and dogwood, paint a gorgeous palette along the banks of the creek. To complement the sight with a splash of green, a random fir tree appears amidst its deciduous cousins. When we cock our heads back and look upward through the colored canopy, the backdrop of blue pulls the entire vision together.

We confirm that our timing has been fortunate. While some leaves still retain green pigment, others have climaxed and already fallen. Those on the ground are scattered sparsely over some areas and in others blanket our path. Having the creek within a few feet of us also proves ideal, not only for its pleasantly consistent gurgle, but also as a repository for some of that foliage. The aspen leaves that often line the bottom and borders of the stream come with a sparkle of reflected sunbeams, fooling us into thinking we have discovered gold.

Added to the rich mix of hues from the foliage, water, and sky are outcrops of rhyolite perched along the nearby slopes that run down to the creek. In some places the pillars appear as if they are competing with the riparian forest, especially the cottonwoods, for bragging rights in the categories of height, form, and color. The stone spires and cliffs pull our gazes past them and up the steep hillsides. Only then do we notice the scattering of gnarled mountain mahogany amidst the sagebrush.

In one place where the drainage flattens out, the trail disappears into slack water created by another beaver dam. Our improvised route around the pond that has flooded several hundred feet of the path first requires a brief climb up the neighboring slope. After gaining twenty feet in elevation, we then make an unsteady contour across the hillside. The steep incline requires us to hang on to any brush available that might prevent us from sliding into the water.

Before we scramble back down to the trail that emerges from the pond, we rest for a bit and enjoy the view. The skeletons of the drowned trees jutting from the water remind me of our February hike and similar circumstances seen in Sinking Canyon. While this dam and pond were created by animal forces of nature rather than geologic, they are again reminders of that same lesson. The natural world is rarely static.

Thinking about the alterations of the two streams witnessed then and now prompts me to consider a landscape's more predictable transitions. The seasonal stories that include plant and animal characters cannot help but imprint on the psyche. I remember January's hike on frozen ground through a dormant, subdued landscape of gray sagebrush and dried grass. As the sun rose higher, days lengthened and the air and soil warmed, tender grass blades emerged, and tree buds swelled and opened. Animals flew back from winter homes thousands of miles distant or edged out of their burrows excavated only a few feet down. Change that began at such an agonizingly slow pace, at least for us humans, accelerated into an unstoppable push.

Life rushed toward reproducing itself—noise and colors and energy filled the natural world. Chicks and furry babies and blooms and seeds miraculously appeared. Not all thrived or even survived, but those that did carried their encoding into the next generation. And now, with autumn having arrived and the coldest months just ahead, life processes wind down or reverse. Photosynthesis ends, leaves drop, and buds set. Most birds migrate back south, while snow or frozen soil push larger mammals to lower elevations and some smaller ones underground. Insects die off but leave eggs that become next year's offspring.

The day is too glorious not to get reclaimed by the present, however, as the journey continues up Camp Creek. Beth's enthusiasm for the scenery is itself beautiful to behold as she tries to capture each perspective with her cameras. She jockeys for position amidst her subjects, strategically placing the creek and trees and stone and sky into a variety of compositions. A touch of clouds are added here or the foliage-covered path there. One large cottonwood tree makes its own offering to the scene with a sprinkle of leaves that flutter downward. Laughter complements the creek's chatter when a few come to rest on her.

We roam little more than a couple miles from the trailhead before stopping to have lunch on a warm rock outcrop that protrudes from our south-facing hillside. There seems little point in proceeding farther; Beth is content with what she had seen, and I am delighted to witness her in the midst of it all. And I will have the chance to experience this corridor again next weekend when I hike through it twice, up and back, on my final trek deep into the mountains.

But other than recognizing I will return soon, there is not much space for thoughts about the future. This gorgeous fall weather and our surroundings offer more than enough to ensure our senses remain fully open and we stay locked in the present. As our stroll proceeds back down the creek, our faces now pointed in the opposite direction, we catch all sorts of new perspectives missed on the way up.

Chapter 18

OCTOBER 18–19

For the third straight weekend I drive through Jackpot, head down Highway 93 for a half hour, and then veer back to the northwest on a gravel road. After reaching the modest rise on the edge of O'Neil Basin, I pull over and study Marys River Peak through my binoculars. The blanket of snow laid across its broad summit several weeks ago has vanished after the pleasant stretch of mild weather. Painted a warm rust color by the rising sun, the peak does not appear very daunting from twenty miles away. I know, however, not to be tricked by appearance. Any landform that rises to over ten thousand feet in elevation takes some effort to get to the top—no matter how its topography might be sculpted.

After getting a sense of the route for my ascent, I drive across the basin, navigate the four-wheel-drive road down to Camp Creek, and park at the trailhead. Within fifteen minutes of carrying my backpack up the path, I again enter the Jarbidge Wilderness Area.

The passage of seven days has taken a toll on the autumn foliage. More leaves now carpet the ground than remain attached to branches, and those that hang on reveal no trace of green pigment. But the trees themselves, especially the aspen, exhibit no less beauty. Stripped of most of their covering, they show off their classic black mottling on white trunks and limbs that stretch into the sky.

While the vegetation is retreating into dormancy, the cooler weather seems to have enticed wildlife out from their hiding places. I first glimpse several doe deer as they wander up the far hillside and later spy an elk looking down from an elevated vantage point. The yearling keeps an eye on me and then strolls off into a small grove of firs after I move underneath and past her.

The most enjoyment comes from seeing a beaver as I finish negotiating the detour around the flooded trail. While there is no way to know if he might be both the design engineer and laborer responsible for the dam and pond, I give him a quiet salute. In turn he rewards me with an entertaining show while I remain hidden behind a couple of near-bare aspens. Using his oversized tail as a rudder, he swims in graceful arcs across the water and through patches of drowned trees. It becomes difficult to watch him without applying human-centric descriptions to his demeanor like casual, contented, or without a care; he just looks like he is having fun. As the animal begins another loop toward the opposite bank, I slip away and leave him undisturbed.

I pause briefly at the place where Beth and I turned around the previous weekend. Besides feeling excited about exploring some new country again, I take a few moments to ponder my arrival at the halfway point in elevation gain between the Snake River and where I hope to summit tomorrow. For some reason I find it amusing that I had to cover 95 percent of the drainage's length, and commit nearly that much in time, to arrive at this spot.

As if to help prove that fact's significance, the gradient of the creek steepens and its water begins to look and sound more animated. For a while the gorge becomes so narrow and restricted that the trail and creek must often trade positions. Each crossing requires care as I step across dry boulders or splash through shallow water flowing over slippery cobble. A little top-heavy from carrying a backpack, I likely have more of a chance falling here along the creek than during the climb tomorrow.

After a sharp bend in the drainage, the small canyon opens up and I follow the trail as it leaves the creek and heads into a small basin. A Forest Service wilderness ranger told me earlier in the week of a trail junction, a perennial spring, and the likelihood of a hunting camp somewhere in the vicinity. None of the spots are hard to find.

Shortly after taking the right fork that keeps me in the Camp Creek drainage, I meet a man striding from a grove of aspens and toward the sound of laughter. After we exchange a quick hello as our paths cross, I hear him mutter, "Now what's going on?" By his demeanor I assume he works as a guide for the Cottonwood Ranch that holds outfitter rights to this portion of the Jarbidge Mountains. Since the trail underneath my feet loops toward the camp, I end up following him.

Greetings are again extended to several hunters. All sporting fresh beards, the men appear to have been out in the woods for a while. While having never participated in a hunting camp but for one time, enough conversation and reading have informed me about the experience of pursuing big game during the day and then convening later to eat, drink, and tell stories. There is no denying a camaraderie forms during these trips, and the realization comes quickly that I am not part of it.

In addition to being the odd man out, my arrival has come at an inopportune time. Several hunters stride in my direction carrying mule deer antlers and then place them on a log lying next to me. When the men themselves begin to line up behind the prone tree, I finally understand that I am in the way of a photo op. I congratulate them on their success, excuse myself, and continue up the trail.

The initial plan for my overnight stay consisted of pitching a tent in the small basin. The flat open area would allow me to enjoy the sun a little longer into the evening rather than being butted up against the base of Marys River Peak. After discovering my first option would put me within a quarter mile of the hunting camp, however, I decide to put a little more space between us. When experiencing wild places, the desire for privacy usually wins out. And I know that doesn't just apply to me, but to most of us that choose to leave our vehicles at the end of the road and walk. The search for our piece of nature absent of other humans is one of the reasons that draw us to these areas in the first place.

The recognition that people need to occasionally escape the civilized world and lose themselves in a large chunk of nature helped lead to the passage of the Wilderness Act of 1964. In the legislation's 156-word definition of wilderness, certain phrases have always resonated with me: "affected primarily by the forces of nature, with the imprint of man's work substantially unnoticeable . . . opportunities for solitude . . . man himself is a visitor who does not remain." As the previous month marked the fiftieth anniversary of that landmark legislation, those criteria possess even more relevance as I walk deeper into the Jarbidge Mountains.

Becoming captivated by Wilderness with a capital *W* feels more meaningful than the two wilderness study areas that I passed through this year. They each possessed unique merits, especially the Bad Lands, but without that official label it doesn't feel quite the same. Yes, I do recognize a bit of snobbery within me. But when enough concerned citizens come together with energy and passion and compromise to protect something special, I feel the need to celebrate them and that inspiring environment. And the irony is not lost on me that the people I often find in wilderness who share that love of landscape are the same visitors that I might shy away from. And I would expect them to also want to keep me at a distance.

And so with that desire for less humanity and more wildness, I allow the country to pull me deeper and higher into its realm. A mile past the spike camp the path returns to Camp Creek. Near where they intersect one last time—by my count this is the twenty-fourth stream crossing—I let the backpack fall to the ground. It will remain here at the mountain's flank, at an elevation of 8,600 feet, and not be carried a single inch higher. As for the summit, it's up there somewhere but remains hidden.

With little reason to proceed farther today, I tend to the task of making camp. The tent is pitched in a rare flat spot near the creek, which before vanishing into the mixture of gravel and sand and then reappearing fifty yards downstream, consists of only a trickle.

Two hours before true sunset, I am shocked at the sight of the sun beginning to slip behind the ridge that towers over me. Not willing to lose its glow this early and already feeling chilled since much physical exertion has ended, I jog up the trail ahead of the sun's oncoming shadow. According to the map, the route makes a dozen switchbacks up a hillside that will lead me away from my mountain and its obstructive ridge. While I won't hike to the top of the saddle—that will happen tomorrow morning—I do enjoy the freedom of walking without a backpack and having the chance to remain in the sunlight's warmth a bit longer.

I play a game for the next twenty minutes that entails racing up one or two switchbacks and then basking in the sunlight as my pursuer almost catches me. I then take on another segment before stopping again. The chase continues until the climb of the shadow accelerates to the point that I have to admit defeat. With no more entertainment available to me except for the book lying in my tent, I remain high on the hillside and watch the light fade from the land. I sit in the midst of the silent world until the cold seeping through my clothes nudges me to get moving again.

After returning to camp, a pang of regret is felt about not bringing a stove and a small pot. The thought of not having anything warm to eat prompts me to review my decision at home the night before. Since cooked meals had not been a part of this year's overnighters, there seemed no reason to concede to that option on this final adventure. Looking back now, I cannot follow my logic. Did I not foresee how cold it would be tonight?

Another activity refrained from during my previous outings also comes to mind—building a fire. "No problem there," I say to myself as the search begins for my matches. With little evidence that anyone has made camp here, I have no trouble gathering a decent stockpile of dry sticks and branches. As the fire grows and my hands warm, the need for anything else fades away and my mind goes blank as I stare into the flames. At some point the trance is broken by the pop of an ember that escapes the small blaze and shoots upward toward the heavens. It is only then that I notice the stars that have taken over the sky. Later, after the fire dies out but before I crawl into the tent, I look up into the Milky Way. At this altitude and degree of seclusion that ensures no competition from artificial light, the flood of starlight amazes me.

After passing seven hours of confinement in a sleeping bag and tent, I cannot remain prone any longer. My hips hurt, my back aches, and a chill has infiltrated my toes. Part of the motivation to escape is also that hiking to the top of a mountain always brings excitement. A few miles to the north I have ascended five others in this mountain range during two separate outings. I cannot help but wonder about the view from the sixth. That I have looked forward to this day ever since my adventure began to take shape also stirs me. The finale has arrived.

After washing down a snack with slushy water, I begin walking at five o'clock. Illuminated by a headlamp, the first section of switchbacks has a different look and feel compared to what I charged up the previous afternoon. Heading north takes me away from my target, which rises to the west, but the difference in direction reflects the motto, especially applicable in the mountains, that progress rarely occurs in a straight line. In this case the steep path will place me on a saddle between two ridges: one that leads to my destination and another that eventually ascends to Gods Pocket Peak. It's a circuitous route, but the best one revealed after a search of the topo map.

It takes about an hour to reach the saddle, where I am forced to pause. The trail followed since yesterday morning drops down into the black void of another drainage—the Jarbidge River's East Fork. The course taken now will be of my choosing that entails a cross-country scramble. Feelings of both anticipation and apprehension about climbing the mountain by myself, along with not having a more defined approach, put me a little on edge. It's not a bad feeling, exactly, but one that makes me cautious about proceeding in the dark.

While trying to keep warm by doing a few exercises, I look to the heavens. Ursa Major, or the Big Dipper, hangs suspended in a position that allows few drops to spill. I follow the outer edges of its cup that point to the North Star and the attached Ursa Minor. I cannot recognize or name many other stars or constellations, but it makes no difference. The view up here, far less obstructed than the one last night tucked away in the deep ravine, takes in an incredible amount of sky. As I try to absorb the sheer number and depth of twinkling lights, I feel small, but somehow centered. The concept of infinity has never seemed more plausible.

When the eastern sky begins to lighten, I leave the saddle and begin a cautious ascent. It's too cold to wait much longer, and the headlamp can stay on as long as needed. As I begin to probe upward my heart beats faster, but the increase is not just about heading uphill in thin air—anxiety and excitement add to the mix. While not overly dangerous, the terrain demands respect and awareness of each connection between land and feet and an occasional hand.

My body thoroughly warms within ten minutes of beginning the ascent. As I move upward the earth continues to rotate, prompting the stars to disappear. After switching my headlamp off, I encounter several rock outcrops that thrust out from the spine of the ridge. A couple of them block my way and require detours. Once the crest begins to flatten out and offers more-stable footing, I realize the sun is lifting above the horizon behind me. Its low angle casts the country in a dramatic contrast. Either the rays strike the sides of the surrounding mountains with full impact, making them appear redder than they truly are, or the shadowed sides remain so dark that no color is perceived. Land little more than ten miles away shows the fuzz of haze built up during the last several weeks of weather dominated by high pressure. The distant, lower elevations of the Snake River Plain and home lie obscured.

After orienting myself with the landscape, I have no need to consult the map and check on my position relative to the mountain's still unseen summit. What's more meaningful right now is that I have arrived at the highest point on this portion of the Salmon Falls Creek watershed.

This tip of the drainage shares boundaries with two others along the ridge that I will continue to climb. On one side I stand over the headwaters of the East Fork of the Jarbidge River, its north slope still harboring patches of snow left over from a late September storm. After this tributary joins forces with the main branch and then flows into the Bruneau, their water finally empties into the Snake River eighty miles to the north. During their journey across the high desert, both of those iconic rivers cut an even deeper set of canyons than the one shaped by Salmon Falls Creek. After turning around and looking south, I peer into the edge of the Great Basin that encompasses nearly all of Nevada and slips into four other states. Below my feet the birth of Marys River will combine with other tributaries to form the Humboldt River—a watershed destined to never reach the ocean.

My focus returns to Camp Creek. I trace the V that it cuts up through the mountains and relive the trek made yesterday. After using binoculars to locate the speck of my tent far below me, I am moved to take stock of my arrival. The desire to reach a high-elevation source to my creek became a constant piece of the motivation for this year's journey. And now that I am here, it suddenly feels necessary to honor the location of its apex.

But I'd like to first find that spot which is shared by those other two drainages. In theory it exists as the point where a single raindrop might fall or snowflake melt and split and run off in three different directions. After making several concentric circles that narrow down the search to about the size of a basketball court, I get down on my hands and knees. When that position offers nothing definitive, I drop to my stomach in hopes of obtaining a closer feel for any sort of slight rise in the micro-terrain. Steeper angles to the ridge would make the search easier, but they don't exist. It's just too flat. I give up, roll over on my back, and look up into the sky.

After contemplating the fall of that exceptional raindrop capable of division, I return to my hands and knees. While there I gather and place three fist-sized rocks on top of each other where the drainages might share common ground. Since no one else is around to check my work and question my choice, I consider the task complete.

Stepping back from the monument, I accept that the elevation here is still nearly four hundred feet lower than Salmon Falls Creek's highest point on Gods Pocket. After first choosing that summit as my destination, I realize that I tricked myself into thinking it was also part of my destiny. The importance attached to Gods Pocket was probably more about ego and bragging rights than anything else. And perhaps that goal was a little too obvious. This miniscule tower of rocks seems more fitting and gives me a sense of satisfaction and a bond to the mountainside.

The walking resumes with less than a mile to cover but seven hundred feet in elevation needed to reach the summit of Marys River. The near-level profile ends after five minutes and I am left with nowhere to go but up. While there are now no boulders or outcrops to maneuver around, the scree and soil set at such a steep angle provide an almost liquid landscape. My hands clutch whatever might be available to prevent me from sliding back down with the flowing earth. Progress comes slowly as my heart thumps like crazy. The effort and elevation force me to stop often.

Eventually the slope tapers off and I accelerate toward a small knoll. The topo map shows the rise is not the actual summit, but I am still gratified to make its acquaintance and catch my breath. After putting a couple of layers of clothing back on for protection against the wind whipping over the bare slope, I hike a slight incline over the final quarter mile.

Ignorant to the rewards of standing on top of a ten-thousand-footer, I did not ascend one until reaching my mid-forties. A decade after climbing Jarbidge Peak, now only a handful of miles away, my feet and legs have propelled me to the summits of a couple dozen lofty mountains. The feel of each arrival is consistent: Relief from not having to push upward anymore. Fulfillment with the accomplishment. Fascination at an unobstructed view in all directions. These merits all meet me on the summit of Marys River Peak. While the panorama is hampered a bit by the haze that dominates the horizon, it still won't be forgotten. My position puts me in almost a perfect line with a string of five peaks that comprise most of the Jarbidge crest. I have never seen nor heard of another alignment that might come close to comparison.

The mountains impress me, but they don't hold my attention for as long as expected. I realize it's not about having seen this lineup twice from the other end, but because my journey has ended. I look down the length of the Camp Creek canyon again, this time following its downstream course. My focus then crosses O'Neil Basin to the Bad Lands and then stretches out to the Granite Range stacked up on the eastern horizon. I strain to see something familiar in Idaho, knowing full well that even on a clear day the narrow canyon corridor that Beth and I shadowed is much too far away. Their images, however, still exist in my mind—it's impossible to move across the earth at a top speed of two miles per hour and not retain indelible prints of particular scenes. Everything I now experience by sight, or my recall, helps me to acknowledge that this is no ordinary summit. It is the culmination of a ten-month exploration and celebration of a stream that has held a place in my heart for most of my life.

After I sign the summit register—only one other soul made the ascent this year—and read entries by other peak-baggers over the years, there is nothing left but to move on. In two days this mountain range will likely receive another blanket of snow, some of which will probably not leave this peak until next spring. With its window for visitation about to close, I offer my gratitude for being able to fit into this landscape. Like with most wild places, the experience is only awarded on a temporary basis—and my time here is over. All that remains is to ease down the mountain, drop back into Salmon Falls Creek's drainage, and find my way home.

ACKNOWLEDGMENTS

While I believe that the project of exploring Salmon Falls Creek would have eventually happened regardless of the circumstances, the telling of this story might not have materialized without the outdoor editor for the Twin Falls Times-News. Thank you, Virginia Hutchins, for your support in allowing me to share some of it first in the form of a 5-part series in 2014.

The actual treks certainly would not have occurred without a large amount of logistical support. Nearly all the outings required a family member to either deliver me somewhere, and at times Beth, or perform a retrieval. Many thanks go to Beth, Keegan, Mom, Leah, and Leon. Local knowledge is vital in trying to wrap one's arms around any type of landscape. Special thanks to Kelly Murphey for sharing his knowledge about the Ancient Ones and to Shawn Willsey for his insight on the forces that shaped the region. Thanks to Joe Gellings, Karen Quinton, Shawna and Zeke Robinson, Agee Smith, and the late Rich Yankey for sharing their stories, and to Rich Bupp for pointing me in the direction of Player Canyon.

Nearly all the ground I traipsed over is managed by the federal government. Nancy Taylor, Jeff Ross, Max Yingst, Blaine Potts, and others who I might have missed—your roles as public servants and the information you provided are much appreciated.

And finally, the endeavor of self-publishing is itself an adventure and obtaining outside expertise a must. Thanks to copyeditor Elissa Curcio for polishing up the manuscript and to Steve Kuhn for the wonderful cover and interior design. In addition to helping make the final product something that brings me plenty of satisfaction, I also learned a few things along the way.

REFERENCES AND SUGGESTED READINGS

Crosswaite, E. G. "Water Resources of Salmon Falls Creek Basin, Idaho-Nevada." Geological Survey Water-Supply Paper 1879-D. Washington, DC: United States Government Printing Office, 1969.

Demo, Pam, and Lee Bennett. "Planning for Paradise—Idaho's Salmon Falls Dam." *Arti-Facts* (Idaho Historical Society) 25, no. 2 (2008).

Dorsch, Steven J. "The Geologic Framework, Movement History, and Mechanics of the Salmon Falls Landslide, Twin Falls County." Master's thesis, Idaho State University, 2004.

Gould, Russell T., and Mark G. Plew. "Prehistoric Salmon Fishing in the Northern Great Basin: Ecological Dynamics, Trade-Offs, and Foraging Strategies." In *Prehistoric Hunter-Gatherer Fishing Strategies*, edited by Mark G. Plew. Boise, ID: Boise State University, 1996.

Hall, Shawn. *Old Heart of Nevada: Ghost Towns and Mining Camps of Elko County*. Reno: University of Nevada Press, 1998.

Lovin, Hugh. "How Not to Run a Carey Act Project: The Twin Falls–Salmon Falls Creek Tract, 1904–1922." *Idaho Yesterdays* 29 (Fall 1986).

Murphey, Kelly, M. J. Freeman, and Peter Bowler. *Valley of the Mighty Snake: An Overview of the Cultural and Natural History of Hagerman Valley, Southwestern Idaho*. Hagerman, ID: Hagerman Valley Historical Society, 1993.

Pasini, Donald J. *Water and American Government: The Reclamation Bureau, National Water Policy, and the West, 1902–1935*. Berkeley and Los Angeles: University of California Press, 2002.

Patterson, Edna B., Louise A. Ulph, and Victor Goodwin. *Nevada's Northeast Frontier*. Sparks, NV: Western Printing and Publishing Company, 1969.

Praggastic, Alissa, and Jack E. Williams. "Salmon's Presence in Nevada's Past." *Nevada Historical Society Quarterly* 56 (Spring/Summer 2013).

Quinton, Karen. *Life in the Saddle on the South Idaho Desert*. Self-published, 1988.

Reisner, Marc. *Cadillac Desert: The American Desert and Its Disappearing Water*. New York: Penguin Books, 1993.

Shallot, Todd, ed. *Secrets of the Magic Valley and Hagerman's Remarkable Horse*. Boise, ID: Black Canyon Communications, 2002.

Steward, Julian H. *Basin-Plateau Aboriginal Sociopolitcal Groups*. Bureau of American Ethnology Bulletin No. 120. Washington, DC: Smithsonian Institution, 1938.

Sweeney, Les. *Henry Harris, 1865–1937: Legendary Black Vaquero*. Payette, ID: C & L Kitchen Table Publishing, 2019.

Wagner, Tricia Martineau. *Black Cowboys of the Old West: True, Sensational, and Little-Known Stories from History*. Guilford, CT: TwoDot, an imprint of Globe Pequot Press, 2010.

Willsey, Shawn. *Geology Underfoot in Southern Idaho*. Missoula, MT: Mountain Press Publishing Company, 2017.

www.ingramcontent.com/pod-product-compliance
Lightning Source LLC
Chambersburg PA
CBHW022053020426
42335CB00012B/671